# Architecture and AI
## Controlling the Hallucination

**Mustapha El Moussaoui**
Bolzano
Italy

CRC Press
Taylor & Francis Group
Boca Raton London New York

CRC Press is an imprint of the
Taylor & Francis Group, an **informa** business
A SCIENCE PUBLISHERS BOOK

*Cover credit*: The image used on the cover is designed by the author.

First edition published 2026
by CRC Press
2385 NW Executive Center Drive, Suite 320, Boca Raton FL 33431

and by CRC Press
4 Park Square, Milton Park, Abingdon, Oxon, OX14 4RN



*CRC Press is an imprint of Taylor & Francis Group, LLC*



*Library of Congress Cataloging-in-Publication Data (applied for)*

ISBN: 978-1-041-06704-7 (hbk)
ISBN: 978-1-041-06895-2 (pbk)
ISBN: 978-1-003-63769-1 (ebk)

DOI: 10.1201/9781003637691

Typeset in Palatino Linotype
by Prime Publishing Services

In the name of the Most Merciful, the Most Powerful.
Dedicated to the long Awaited
my Mother and Father

# Preface

Imagine the year is 1380. You stand beneath the vaults of a cathedral in France. Scaffolds cling to the walls like a second city above the floor. The Master Mason directs the work with a glance and a gesture. His knowledge lives in tools, in calloused muscle memory, in guarded rules of thumb passed through the guild. He designs at the pace of stone. His authority rests on embodied expertise that only the builders can read.

Then a courier arrives from Italy with a roll of parchment. On it: a façade rendered in linear perspective, accompanied by measurements and notes. It is not only an image. It is an abstraction, a portable package of intention. For the first time a patron can look at a project as a whole, compare it with others, approve or reject it, even commission work far from the site of building. To the Master Mason this looks like sterile theory. To a new kind of patron it looks like transparency, even control.

The market shifts. It allow decisions to be made away from the scaffold, in counting houses and councils. The master who refuses the new abstraction is not defeated in debate. He is displaced by a new medium that changes how architecture is coordinated and financed.

This is not a romantic parable. It is a reminder that new technologies do more than depict. They restructure who decides, who pays, and who is accountable.

In 2022 diffusion models moved from labs into everyday use and architectural representation changed almost overnight. A short prompt produced images that once required modeling, rendering, and patient iteration. The gain was real. So was the risk. Velocity can separate output from intention. From that moment my question was concrete. How do we keep architectural judgment inside tools that can easily run ahead of us.

My formation sits on two pillars. I was trained to read architecture phenomenologically, with attention to how light, sound, material, and scale support lived experience. I was also trained to compute. I wrote scripts, built simulations, and used data to test design claims. Which some might call post-phenomenology. These are not rival commitments. They are complementary ways of reasoning about space. The task is to hold them together so that the calculable serves the habitable.

The diffusion turn exposed a gap between representation and authorship. Students produced convincing images in minutes and then asked if those images still belonged to them. Were the models only instruments, or did they now function as coauthors. In parallel, offices reorganized around new pipelines faster than university programs could revise syllabi. The lesson was not to chase novelty. It was to teach posture. Agency must be maintained when representation accelerates.

I began with a course I knew well. For years I had taught Descriptive Geometry and Spatial Composition in its classical sequence. Orthographic projection, axonometric construction, section, and shadow. The discipline matters because it forces explicit statements about what is known and what is inferred. I kept that sequence and placed a second sequence beside it. We opened the generative tools we were already using. We asked how data becomes a prior, how noise becomes signal through sampling, how a seed stabilizes exploration, how control inputs steer a distribution, and how bias enters through training sets. We learned to diagnose a failed image by tracing it back through its pipeline. This was not training architects to become machine learning engineers. It was removing mystique so that authorship could be argued and defended.

Outside the classroom the pressures were similar. Competitions rewarded speed. Clients expected early designs that looked resolved. Colleagues asked how to integrate new models without letting them dictate taste. I taught workshops, built small installations, and wrote articles on Artificial Intelligence.

Here the medieval scene becomes useful again. Perspective did not destroy craft. It formalized intention and made complex work coordinable across distance and time. It also shifted power. Those who learned to draw gained power. Those who refused it kept skill but lost direction. In history it is always clear, those who create and use technologies sit on the throne of power. Artificial Intelligence is the present version of that shift. They can expand perception, accelerate iteration, and widen the search space. They can also mask intention, entrench bias, and reward spectacle if used uncritically. The question is not adoption. The question is governance. Who specifies, who constrains, who validates, and by what criteria.

This is the point at which the book became necessary. A set of lectures was not enough. Students need a structured way to connect geometric literacy with generative literacy. Educators need a path to modernize foundations without discarding them. Practitioners need protocols that integrate new tools without lowering standards. Researchers need a vocabulary that allows architectural theory, human computer interaction, and machine learning to meet on technical ground.

Why we need technology follows directly from this history. Abstractions like drawing, simulation, and generation are not decorations on top of making. They are the means by which intention becomes communicable, testable, and contractible. It is a language. They let us see consequences before they harden into concrete and cost. They allow collaboration at scale. They give students and offices a larger search space and a tighter feedback loop. We need them to reduce error, to price risk, to coordinate labor, and to measure claims about comfort, performance, and care. We need them to widen our imagination without losing responsibility.

The risk is not the existence of new tools. The risk is using them passively. The Master Mason lost when he refused the new language of representation. We will lose authorship if we refuse to learn how generative systems reason and how they can be steered. The alternative is clear. Treat the model as a material. Specify, constrain, test, and revise. Keep site, climate, and community inside the loop. Pair orthographic rigor with generative exploration. Require that every image answer to life on the ground.

I began writing because I saw the same conversation replayed in many rooms. The tools will continue to change while you read. That is not a problem if the method is stable. What endures is a way of thinking that keeps intention, ethics, and accountability inside computation. This book is an attempt to make that way of thinking teachable and transferable. Control the hallucination. Use technology to extend care, not to replace it. Keep authorship—not in an egoistic approach, but more to keep our existential identities intact- by learning the new language.

# Acknowledgment

I am deeply indebted to many who have supported me in the process of writing this monograph. From its inception, the project required an interdisciplinary approach. Throughout the writing and long before it, I benefited from the generosity and insights of colleagues across the Computer Science Department, the Faculty of Design and Art, and the IT office at the Free University of Bolzano, all of whom patiently engaged with my persistent and, at times, burdening questions. This book has been as much a process of learning as of teaching, and I am grateful for the dialogues that shaped it.

My deepest gratitude goes to my wife, Dana, whose unwavering support, care for our children, and dedication, made it possible for me to bring this work to completion. Without her presence, encouragement, and sacrifice, this book could not have been written.

This research was funded by the European Social Fund Plus, Project Code ESF2_f3_0006, CUP: B56F24000090001, Research projects on strategic topics for the South Tyrolean economy carried out by researchers on fixed-term contracts.

# Contents

# List of Figures

# List of Tables

# Chapter 1

# Introduction

The shadow that fell over the Master Mason in the 14th century was cast by a sheet of parchment. On it, the new technology of disegno—of abstract, rational drawing—projected a vision of a building with perfect, mathematical certainty. It was a tool of immense power that promised speed, predictability, and control, and as we saw, the market's embrace of it was absolute. The Mason who failed to master this new form of abstraction was not defeated; he was demoted, his role shifting from author to executor. Today, a new shadow falls upon our profession. It does not come from parchment, but from the latent space of neural networks, and it does not offer certainty, but its very opposite: hallucination.

This book is about how we, the architects of the 21st century, can learn to master this new shadow. The subtitle, Controlling Hallucination, is chosen with deliberate intent. It frames the central challenge presented by the sudden, explosive rise of Artificial Intelligence in the creative fields. AI, in this context, is not merely a tool for automation, like a more efficient CAD program. It is a fundamental shift in the nature of representation itself. These systems—particularly the generative models that produce images from text and other inputs—do not "think" or "design" in any human sense. They operate through a process of sophisticated, high-dimensional pattern recognition, dreaming up solutions by statistically associating concepts and aesthetics from a vast ocean of data they have been trained on. The results are often beautiful, startling, and uncannily plausible. But they are also arbitrary. They are visions without intention.

This brings us to a moment of profound professional anxiety, one anticipated with remarkable prescience by Richard and Daniel Susskind. In their 2015 book, The Future of the Professions, they argued that the role of the professional as a gatekeeper of specialized knowledge was coming to an end. They predicted that intelligent systems would eventually automate the core tasks of fields like medicine, law, and architecture. A radiologist's diagnostic eye could be replaced by an algorithm trained

DOI: 10.1201/9781003637691-1

on millions of scans; a lawyer's document review by a system that never tires; an architect's design and documentation process by a tool that could manage a project from conception to completion.

When their book was published, this future felt distant. By 2021, the dramatic disruption they forecast had not fully materialized, particularly in architecture, a profession historically insulated by its complexity and its slow adoption of new technologies. But this lag was not a sign of immunity; it was merely the quiet before the storm. The recent advent of powerful, accessible generative models has shattered that quiet. The Susskinds' prophecy is no longer a theoretical debate; it is a practical reality knocking at the door, and its arrival is being accelerated by the same market forces that embraced the paper architect centuries ago: the relentless demand for work to be faster, cheaper, and more visually immediate.

The danger, however, is more subtle than simple replacement. It is, as the Master Mason's story warns, the danger of demotion. If architects become mere prompters—whispering suggestions to a machine and then curating the most appealing of its random hallucinations—we abdicate our primary role. Architecture is, at its essence, a discipline of radical intentionality. It is the art and science of solving complex, overlapping problems—functional, structural, environmental, social, and aesthetic—through a series of deliberate, reasoned decisions. An arbitrary solution, no matter how beautiful, is a failure of this core mandate.

This is why we must learn to control the hallucination. The goal is not to eliminate the generative capacity of AI, but to build a scaffold of constraints and feedback loops around it. It is to move from being a passive audience to its dreams to becoming the active director of its generative power. This requires a fundamental rethinking of our design process. It demands a new kind of architectural literacy, one that is as fluent in the logic of neural networks as it is in the language of form and space.

This necessary evolution is being hampered by a critical vulnerability: our own systems of education. Architectural pedagogy, often led by professionals from a pre-generative era, has been slow to integrate these emerging paradigms. If educators themselves are struggling to learn and adapt to these tools, teaching them effectively becomes an even greater challenge. This educational lag creates a dangerous vacuum, leaving the next generation of architects ill-equipped for the most significant technological shift since the dawn of digital design.

Therefore, this book is structured as both a theoretical map and a practical manual for this new territory. It is designed to guide you, the reader, through the evolving relationship between AI and architecture, from foundational concepts to hands-on application.

First, we will demystify the machine. We will explore the core principles of AI, machine learning, and the specific neural network architectures—like Generative Adversarial Networks (GANs) and Diffusion Models—

that have become so instrumental in creative generation. Understanding how these models are trained, how they "learn" from data, and how they generalize that learning is the essential first step toward controlling their output.

Having established this conceptual foundation, the book will pivot to a practical, hands-on focus on ComfyUI, an accessible, open-source tool that allows for an unparalleled degree of control over the AI image generation pipeline. This section is not a simple software tutorial. It is a digital workshop. With detailed, step-by-step guidance, we will deconstruct the generative process, learning how to manipulate every variable to guide the AI away from arbitrary results and toward architecturally coherent and intentional outcomes. You will learn to generate images, create consistent animations, and integrate these tools into a rigorous design workflow, transforming AI from a generator of random novelty into a disciplined, powerful collaborator.

The lesson of the Master Mason is not that technology is a threat, but that a failure to master the dominant tools of abstraction leads to a loss of authorship. This book is a call for architects to seize this new technology, to bend it to our will, and to use it to elevate our discipline, ensuring that we remain the indispensable visionaries of the built environment, not the mere operators of the machines that dream it into existence.

# Part 1

## Theoretical Foundations

# Chapter 2

# Introduction to AI

In the introduction, I mentioned: before we can learn to control the machine's hallucination, we must first understand the nature of the machine itself. We must peer inside the new shadow that has fallen over our profession, not with fear, but with the focused curiosity of a craftsman examining a new and powerful tool. This chapter, therefore, is our journey into the black box. We will demystify Artificial Intelligence, stripping away the layers of science fiction and technical jargon to reveal the elegant, and surprisingly simple, principles that give it its power.

To begin, we must discard the popular metaphor of AI as an "artificial brain." While convenient, it is misleading. A brain comprehends, feels, and possesses consciousness. The forms of AI that concern us do none of these things. It is more accurate to think of AI not as a new kind of mind, but as a new kind of engine. The steam engine converted thermal energy into mechanical force, driving the Industrial Revolution. The computer, in its first incarnation, was an engine for logic, executing pre-programmed instructions with perfect fidelity. The AI of today is a third type of engine: it is an engine for inference. It does not run on steam or logic, but on data. Its function is to ingest a vast quantity of information and infer the hidden patterns, relationships, and probabilities within it. The "hallucination" of a generative model is the exhaust of this engine—a statistically plausible output based on the patterns it has learned.

This idea of an intelligent, non-human creation is not new. It is a dream as old as civilization itself. The myths of antiquity are filled with such beings: the Golem of Prague, molded from clay and brought to life by esoteric words; the bronze automaton Talos, forged by the god Hephaestus to guard the shores of Crete. These stories reveal a deep and ancient human yearning to breathe life into the inanimate, to create a mirror to our own intelligence. For centuries, however, this remained the stuff of legend. The formal journey toward a true thinking machine began much later, as a problem of philosophy and mathematics.

DOI: 10.1201/9781003637691-3

It was the 17th-century polymath Gottfried Wilhelm Leibniz who first dreamed of a universal language of reason, the *characteristica universalis*, which could reduce all human thought to precise calculation. If such a language existed, he reasoned, then a machine could be built to manipulate its symbols and resolve any argument. Two centuries later, Charles Babbage designed his Analytical Engine, a mechanical computer that, had it been built, would have been the physical embodiment of this dream—a machine that could follow logical instructions. Yet these were still engines of logic. They required a human author to write their every instruction. They could calculate, but they could not *learn*.

The true conceptual birth of modern AI occurred in 1950, in a paper by the British mathematician Alan Turing. In "Computing Machinery and Intelligence," he swept aside the philosophical baggage of asking "Can machines think?" and replaced it with a practical, operational question: Can a machine behave in a way that is indistinguishable from a human? The famous Turing Test was not just a clever thought experiment; it was a profound reframing of the problem. It suggested that intelligence was not an ethereal essence, but a quality of performance that could be engineered (Fig. 1).

Six years later, at a summer conference at Dartmouth College, the discipline was officially christened. The term "artificial intelligence" was coined, and its pioneers laid out a vision of staggering ambition. Their initial approach, now known as "Symbolic AI" or "Good Old-Fashioned AI (GOFAI)," was a direct descendant of Leibniz's dream. It was based on the idea that human knowledge could be broken down into a vast web of facts and rules. Early triumphs of this era, like Newell and Simon's Logic Theorist (1956), which could prove mathematical theorems, and their subsequent General Problem Solver (GPS), which attempted to mimic human problem-solving strategies, created a wave of optimism. This culminated in the 1970s with the rise of "expert systems." These were programs designed to be specialists in a narrow domain, such as DENDRAL for chemical analysis or MYCIN for diagnosing blood infections. They operated on a large, hand-crafted database of rules provided by human experts, and for a time, they seemed to fulfill the promise of AI.

But this paradigm had a fatal flaw. For decades, it produced some successes in constrained environments, but it ultimately hit a wall. The world, it turned out, was too messy, too ambiguous, and too complex to be captured in a finite set of human-written rules. The reliance on hand-crafted knowledge was brittle; these systems had no common sense and could not function outside their narrow expertise. This led to a period of disillusionment in the 1980s known as the "AI Winter," when unmet expectations led to funding cuts and slowed research.

During this winter, however, a different idea was gaining traction, one inspired not by logic, but by biology: connectionism, and its primary

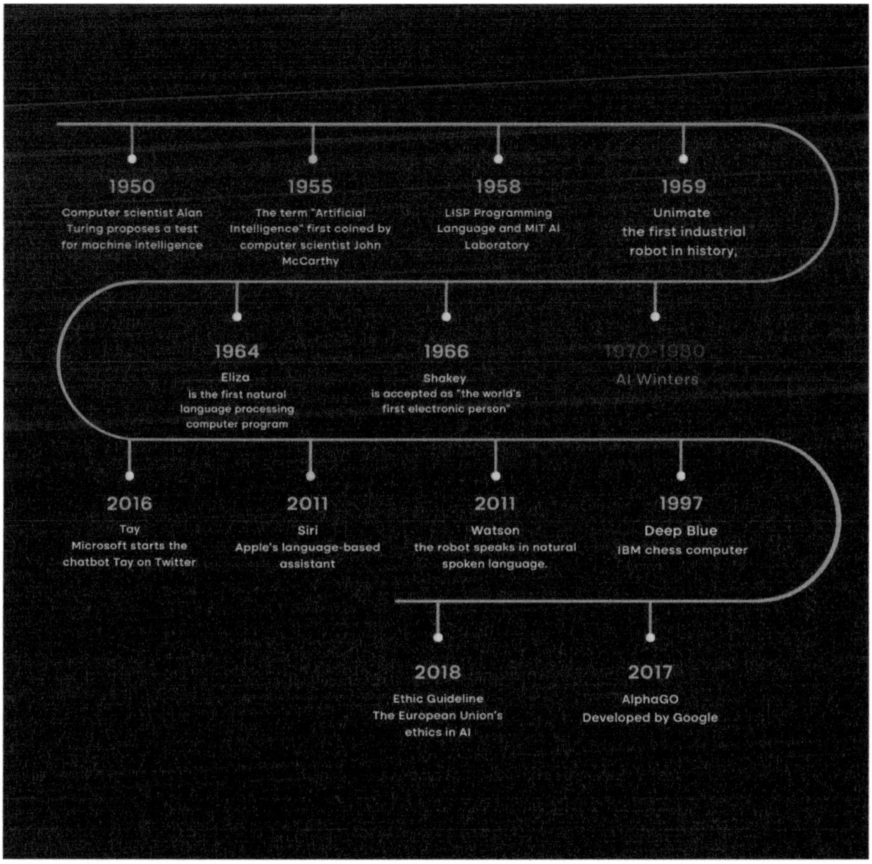


**Figure 1.** A figure showing the chronological advances of AI (Formica, 2023).

tool, the neural network. Instead of programming a machine with rules, what if you could create a system that learned the rules on its own, simply by observing examples? This is the core of machine learning, the subfield of AI that powers today's generative revolution. The rediscovery of a crucial training algorithm called backpropagation in 1986 by researchers including Geoffrey Hinton was a key moment, laying the groundwork for what was to come.

The true resurgence began in the 2000s, driven by a perfect storm: the exponential growth of computational power (as described by Moore's Law), the availability of vast datasets from the internet, and increasingly sophisticated algorithms. The paradigm shifted decisively from rule-based programming to data-driven learning. A breakthrough occurred in 2012 when a deep Convolutional Neural Network (CNN) called AlexNet, developed by Alex Krizhevsky, Geoffrey Hinton, and Ilya Sutskever, achieved a stunning victory in the ImageNet competition, an annual challenge to classify images. AlexNet's unprecedented accuracy demonstrated the power of deep learning at a massive scale and triggered the modern AI boom.

This led to a Cambrian explosion of new architectures. The development of Generative Adversarial Networks (GANs) by Ian Goodfellow in 2014 was another pivotal moment, giving AI the astounding ability to generate novel, realistic images and data. Today, these systems power everything from autonomous vehicles to the large language models that have captured the public imagination.

This brings us directly back to hallucination. When we ask a generative AI to create an image of "a brutalist library on Mars," it is not logically reasoning about what a library is or what Mars looks like. It is tapping into its vast, abstract model of concepts, a model built through the connectionist approach of learning from data. It dredges up the statistical patterns associated with "brutalism" (raw concrete, massive forms), "library" (shelves, light, reading spaces), and "Mars" (red desert, thin atmosphere), and it synthesizes a new image that is a plausible blend of all those learned patterns. It is dreaming in the language of data. The dream may be beautiful, but it is unreasoned. Our task, as we will see in the chapters to come, is to become the architects of those dreams.

## Data: From the Alphabet to AI—The Hidden Architecture of Intelligence

In the last chapter, we traced the evolution of the artificial mind, following its journey from an engine of logic to an engine of inference. We saw how the dream of AI shifted from painstakingly programming rules into a machine to creating a system that could learn on its own. Now, we must turn our attention to the silent partner in this revolution, the single element that makes this learning possible. If AI is the engine, then data is not only its fuel; it is the very landscape the engine traverses, the archive it consults, and, increasingly, the raw material from which it builds.

To truly grasp the transformation unfolding in architecture, we must understand that the story of data does not begin with the silicon chip. It begins with a far more ancient technology: the alphabet. Long before digital computation, writing was the first great act of data compression. It was a system for distilling the boundless, fluid, and ephemeral nature of spoken language—rich with intonation, gesture, and presence—into a finite set of discrete, replicable symbols. With this, knowledge was liberated from the fragile confines of human memory. It became portable, durable, and scalable. A thought could now outlive its thinker. This compression, however, came at a cost. Nuance was sacrificed for legibility, and context was stripped away in favor of portability. The living word became a flat mark on a surface.

Centuries later, the printing press weaponized this principle. If the alphabet made knowledge portable, the press made it viral. Ideas that once required the painstaking labor of scribes could now be mass-produced with mechanical precision, colonizing the minds of a continent. Architecture was profoundly shaped by this explosion. Treatises from Vitruvius to Palladio crossed borders, canonizing formal styles and mathematical proportions. A villa designed in rural England could suddenly mirror one in Veneto, not because of direct cultural exchange, but because both architects drew from the same circulated data set of plans and elevations. The drawing became the ultimate instrument of architectural authority, a standardized instruction set for reproducing a design anywhere in the world.

This logic of compression and standardization—of reducing the messy complexity of reality into clean, rule-based, and portable forms—persisted well into what the architectural theorist Mario Carpo has termed the "first digital turn." The early era of CAD and parametric design did not fundamentally disrupt this logic; it perfected it. Architects wrote scripts, set parameters, and encoded formal systems into software. The machine, faster and more precise than any human hand, remained a faithful executor of the architect's explicit intentions. It was the apotheosis of the top-down, rule-bound design process that began with the first architectural drawing.

But then, something shifted. As computational power soared and the cost of digital storage plummeted toward zero, the age-old need to compress began to evaporate. The logic of reduction gave way to a new logic of accumulation. We began to save everything. Every photograph, every transaction, every stray thought posted online. In architecture, this meant every 3D scan, every satellite image, every material simulation. Why approximate a historic column with a clean Vitruvian ratio when a LiDAR scanner could capture its every chip, stain, and subtle deviation from the ideal? Why describe reality when you could simply store it in high-resolution?

This is the threshold of Carpo's "second digital turn," the moment we are living through now. It is an era defined not by a poverty of information, but by an overwhelming abundance of it. And it is from this vast, messy, and uncompressed accumulation of data that a new kind of intelligence can emerge.

In the realm of AI, this means that machines no longer require hand-crafted rules. They are not taught what to see; they are simply shown. Feed an algorithm millions of labeled images—"church," "house," "skyscraper"—and it begins to identify statistical regularities on its own. It learns not through deductive logic, but through inductive correlation. It does not understand what a church is in any philosophical sense;

it calculates a high probability that things with towers, arches, and cruciform plans belong to the category "church." Intelligence becomes a function of pattern exposure.

In this new paradigm, the role of the architect is undergoing its most profound shift since the Renaissance. The architect is no longer just a designer of form or a writer of code. Increasingly, they are a curator of data. To design with AI is to first design what the machine sees. The selection of a training set—the decision to include these historical examples but not those, to favor this style over another, to clean the data in a particular way—is no longer a preliminary step. It is a primary act of design.

This transformation brings with it a new set of challenges that are both technical and deeply philosophical. A neural network trained on thousands of images of Gothic cathedrals may hallucinate a structure that "feels" authentically Gothic without adhering to a single historical rule of construction. These designs are not errors; they are statistical aggregates, weighted averages of the data they have consumed. The machine does not reconstruct history; it recomposes its shadow. Creativity becomes a matter of recombinant memory, not singular invention.

Today, data is no longer a passive resource to be consulted. It is an active, epistemological force—a substrate of design thought that shapes what is visible, legible, and ultimately, imaginable. When we curate a dataset, we are not just training a machine; we are embedding our values, our biases, our omissions, and our cultural blind spots into its operational DNA. From the earliest alphabets to the generative models of today, the story of data is the story of how humanity has chosen to externalize, preserve, and manipulate knowledge. In architecture, this story is now revealing itself in the machine's uncanny ability to dream of buildings that have never existed, yet feel eerily, and sometimes beautifully, familiar.

# Chapter 3

# Core Components of AI

## Datasets: Types and Significance in AI

A dataset is the collection of information from which an AI model learns. The quality and structure of a dataset are crucial, as they directly influence the accuracy and reliability of the AI's predictions. Datasets can vary widely in type and format, depending on the task, and they fall into a few main categories:

- **Structured Data**: Organized data with a clear, defined format, often in tables or spreadsheets. Each entry is structured in rows and columns, like a database containing names, addresses, or architectural details (e.g., building height, material type). This format is ideal for tasks like data analysis and prediction since it's easy for algorithms to process (Kelleher, 2019).
- **Unstructured Data**: Unlike structured data, unstructured data doesn't follow a specific format. Examples include images, audio files, videos, and text documents, all of which can vary greatly in size and shape. For instance, a collection of building images with no labels would be considered unstructured. Many AI tasks in architecture, such as image recognition, rely on unstructured data.
- **Labeled Data**: Data where each example includes a label or answer, which tells the AI what it is looking at. For example, in an architectural dataset, images could be labeled with building types ("House," "Office," etc.). Labeled data is essential for *supervised learning* because it guides the AI in recognizing patterns (Goodfellow et al., 2016).
- **Unlabeled Data**: Data without labels, meaning the AI doesn't have predefined answers to learn from. This is used in *unsupervised learning*, where the AI explores the data on its own to find patterns or groupings. For example, if given a large set of building images with

DOI: 10.1201/9781003637691-4

no labels, the AI might group similar architectural styles together based on visual features (Russell and Norvig, 2021).

Datasets are critical because they shape what an AI system learns. If the dataset is biased or incomplete, the AI's understanding will be limited, impacting its ability to generalize. In architecture, high-quality, well-labeled datasets can allow AI to distinguish complex architectural styles or predict the best materials for a given project (Mitchell, 1997).

## Models and Training: How AI Learns from Data

A model in AI is essentially a mathematical structure or "blueprint" that enables the system to process data and make predictions. Models are trained on datasets, which means they "study" the data to identify patterns, relationships, and classifications.

- **Supervised Learning**: In supervised learning, the model learns from labeled data. Each example in the dataset has an input and a correct output. The model is trained by being shown the input-output pairs repeatedly until it can accurately predict the output based on new inputs. For instance, an AI trained with labeled images of buildings can learn to classify architectural styles when shown new, unlabeled images (Goodfellow et al., 2016).
- **Unsupervised Learning**: In unsupervised learning, the AI is given unlabeled data and must identify patterns on its own. This method is useful for tasks where labels are not available, and it's often used for clustering or grouping similar items. For example, an unsupervised model given various architectural images may group them into clusters representing different styles without knowing the specific labels (Kelleher, 2019).
- **Reinforcement Learning**: This type of learning involves an AI agent interacting with an environment to achieve a goal. The agent receives rewards or penalties based on its actions, guiding it toward the optimal strategy. While less common in static architectural tasks, reinforcement learning can be applied in dynamic environments, like optimizing building energy use over time (Sutton and Barto, 2018).

The training process involves feeding data into the model, allowing it to learn from examples. Initially, the model's predictions may be inaccurate. However, as it sees more data and makes adjustments, it improves its ability to make accurate predictions.

## Optimization and Evaluation: Fine-Tuning AI's Performance

Training doesn't make a model perfect; it requires optimization to improve accuracy and evaluation to ensure reliability. These steps are essential to making sure an AI system works well in real-world tasks.

- **Cost Functions**: During training, the model measures its errors using a cost function, which calculates the difference between the predicted output and the actual label. The goal is to minimize this cost over time, ensuring the model's predictions get closer to the correct answer with each example. Think of the cost function as a way of telling the AI, "How far off were you, and what can you do to improve?"
- **Accuracy**: After training, the model's accuracy is evaluated using a test set. Accuracy measures the percentage of correct predictions, helping assess the model's reliability. High accuracy means the AI has learned well, while low accuracy suggests it might need more training or data adjustments.
- **Generalizability**: A critical aspect of AI performance is generalizability, or the ability of the AI to perform well on new, unseen data. Generalizability ensures the AI isn't just memorizing examples but actually understands the underlying patterns, enabling it to make accurate predictions on unfamiliar data (Mitchell, 1997).

# Chapter 4

# Architectures of Learning

## From Perceptrons to Multimodal Intelligence

Having traversed the foundational terrain of what Artificial Intelligence (AI) is and how it learns, the reader now stands at the threshold of understanding the very architectures- the anatomies- through which AI acquires its astonishing abilities. Just as the structure of a cathedral or a skyscraper dictates its aesthetic, function, and performance, so too do the internal architectures of AI systems dictate their capabilities and limitations.

What follows is not merely a list of technical models, but rather an unfolding narrative of how different approaches to machine learning-structured as distinct architectures- have evolved, how they are related, and why their philosophical and practical significance matters profoundly to designers and architects today.

## The Age of Neurons: Perceptrons and Artificial Neural Networks (ANNs)

The first step towards modern AI architectures began with an attempt to mimic the biological neuron, a structure capable of receiving input, processing it, and transmitting output. As mentioned earlier, the Perceptron, invented by Frank Rosenblatt in 1958, was the earliest such model (Rosenblatt, 1958). However, its simplicity proved both revolutionary and limiting. While it could detect patterns in data, it could only manage linearly separable problems—basic distinctions that could be represented as straight-line divisions.

DOI: 10.1201/9781003637691-5

It was not until the 1980s that the Artificial Neural Network (ANN), capable of more complex, multi-layered learning, came to prominence with the rediscovery of the backpropagation algorithm (Rumelhart, Hinton, & Williams, 1986). ANNs became the conceptual foundation for almost all modern AI models.

ANNs remain the structural skeleton for:

1. **Convolutional Neural Networks (CNNs)** Built on ANNs but specialize in processing grid-like data (e.g., images) using convolutional layers.
2. **Recurrent Neural Networks (RNNs)** ANNs with loops to handle sequential data (e.g., time series, text).
3. **Generative Adversarial Networks (GANs)** Consist of two competing ANNs (a generator and a discriminator).
4. **Transformers (and LLMs)** Use self-attention mechanisms but still rely on ANN-based layers (feedforward networks, embeddings, etc.).
5. **Diffusion Models** Use ANNs (often U-Nets, a CNN variant) to gradually denoise data.
6. **Spatially-aware architectures** Many newer models (e.g., graph neural networks, 3D CNNs) extend ANN principles to specialized domains.

Just as Gothic arches evolved into the skeletal frames of modern skyscrapers, so too has the simple ANN undergirded the increasingly sophisticated architectures to come.

## Seeing Patterns: Convolutional Neural Networks (CNNs)

While traditional Artificial Neural Networks (ANNs) could learn from data, they lacked spatial awareness, a critical limitation for visual tasks. Convolutional Neural Networks (CNNs), pioneered by Yann LeCun in 1989, revolutionized this by introducing convolutional layers. Unlike dense ANNs, which process flattened inputs, these layers scan images locally, detecting hierarchical features (edges → textures → objects) while preserving spatial relationships (LeCun et al., 1989).

CNNs quickly became the gold standard for image recognition, later enabling breakthroughs in architectural applications, from facade style classification to spatial occupancy analysis. Importantly, CNNs are a specialized subtype of ANNs, distinguished by their use of:

- Convolutional filters (shared weights for translation invariance)
- Pooling layers (spatial downsampling)
- Hierarchical feature learning (local-to-global pattern detection)

Though more efficient than dense ANNs for grid-like data, CNNs still rely on core ANN principles (backpropagation, activation functions). Today, they underpin not just computer vision but also video analysis, medical imaging, and even modern generative models (e.g., diffusion models' U-Net architectures).

## Learning Sequences: Recurrent Neural Networks (RNNs) and LSTMs

Architects understand that sequence matters: the unfolding of a spatial experience depends on ordered progression. Similarly, for AI to understand time series, language, or sequential events, it needed an architecture capable of remembering what came before.

Enter Recurrent Neural Networks (RNNs) and their more powerful variant, Long Short-Term Memory (LSTM) networks (Hochreiter and Schmidhuber, 1997). These allowed AI to loop information, maintaining a memory of past inputs while processing new ones.

Although later overshadowed by Transformers, RNNs and LSTMs laid the groundwork for natural language processing (NLP) and time-based data analysis.

## Imagining New Forms: Generative Adversarial Networks (GANs)

In 2014, Ian Goodfellow introduced a radical concept: two neural networks locked in adversarial competition. The Generative Adversarial Network (GAN) consists of a generator (creating new data) and a discriminator (judging whether the data is real or fake) (Goodfellow et al., 2014).

Through iterative competition, the generator improves, producing outputs indistinguishable from real data.

GANs are not a subset of Diffusion Models.

They are a distinct class of generative models. Where GANs rely on adversarial feedback, Diffusion Models use probabilistic processes to iteratively refine noise into meaningful data.

GANs transformed generative design, enabling architects to explore vast solution spaces, from facade variations to urban morphology simulations.

## Understanding Context: The Rise of Transformers and LLMs

In 2017, AI took another conceptual leap with the invention of the Transformer architecture (Vaswani et al., 2017). Its core innovation, self-attention, allowed AI models to weigh the relevance of different parts of input data dynamically.

This architecture powered the emergence of Large Language Models (LLMs):

- GPT-2 (2019)
- GPT-3 (2020)
- GPT-4 (2023)
- and even multimodal successors (2024–2025) like GPT-4o and Gemini 1.5.

Transformers outperformed RNNs and LSTMs, becoming the dominant architecture not only for text but also for images, code, and even spatial data.

## From Noise to Art: Diffusion Models

The next leap came with Diffusion Models, especially Denoising Diffusion Probabilistic Models (DDPM) (Ho et al., 2020) and later Latent Diffusion Models like Stable Diffusion (Rombach et al., 2022).

Unlike GANs, Diffusion Models work by adding noise to data until it becomes meaningless, then learning how to reverse the noise process to generate new data from scratch.

This process proved to be more stable and versatile than GANs, powering modern text-to-image models like DALL·E, Midjourney, and Stable Diffusion.

Key clarification:

Diffusion Models and GANs are both generative, but fundamentally different.

- GANs: Adversarial training.
- Diffusion: Probabilistic denoising.

Diffusion has become the default architecture for generative AI imagery—including architectural visualizations.

## Bridging Senses: Multimodal AI and Vision-Language Models

In 2021, OpenAI's CLIP introduced Contrastive Language-Image Pretraining, aligning text and image representations (Radford et al., 2021). This innovation made it possible for AI to "understand" visual content through natural language—foundational for Midjourney, DALL·E, and similar tools.

By 2024, models like GPT-4o (OpenAI, 2025) advanced multimodal reasoning, allowing seamless understanding of text, image, and spatial data.

## Toward Space: Spatial AI and the Emergence of SpatialGPT

As of 2024–2025, AI has begun to advance beyond 2D perception, explicitly integrating spatial and geometric reasoning into its frameworks. Prototypes like SpatialGPT (Microsoft, 2024) extend the LLM paradigm to 3D data understanding, enabling models to interpret and generate spatial constructs—from volumetric designs to interactive architectural scenarios.

- SpatialGPT: An experimental fusion of LLMs with 3D-aware architectures, capable of parsing and generating spatial relationships (e.g., "Design a room with north-facing windows adjacent to a courtyard").
- Neural Radiance Fields (NeRFs) (Mildenhall et al., 2020): Enable photorealistic 3D scene synthesis from 2D images, critical for virtual reconstructions or pre-visualization.
- Graph Neural Networks (GNNs) (Liang et al., 2025): Model relational geometry (e.g., connectivity between structural elements) for tasks like urban planning or material load analysis.

While still nascent, these technologies hint at a future where AI collaborates in spatial design workflows, automating layout optimizations or generating regulatory-compliant building plans.

# Chapter 5

# Latent Space

## The Cognitive and Computational Foundation of Generative AI in Architecture

Generative artificial intelligence (AI) has profoundly reshaped architecture by transforming how we conceptualize, design, and understand space. Central to this revolution is the latent space- an abstract, computational framework that underpins how AI models learn, process, and generate ideas. The latent space represents a powerful fusion of mathematical principles and cognitive theory, establishing it as an essential foundation for contemporary architectural creativity.

## Understanding Latent Space

At its core, a latent space is a high-dimensional map of concepts created by a generative AI. The model learns to compress complex data- such as images, texts, or architectural forms- into a simplified but meaningful set of coordinates on this map. These coordinates are often called latent vectors.

Instead of grappling with the immense detail of raw data, the AI translates an input into this condensed representation. Think of a latent vector as a distilled summary, efficiently capturing the essential features of an object. This process involves two critical components:

- **The Encoder:** This is a neural network that compresses input data, like an architectural drawing or a building façade, into a compact latent vector. It essentially finds the "address" for that specific design concept on the latent space map.

DOI: 10.1201/9781003637691-6

- **The Decoder:** This is a complementary network that takes a latent vector (an address on the map) and translates it back into a detailed architectural image.

This dual process enables more than mere replication; it allows for controlled exploration and imaginative variations within the boundaries of what the model has learned.

## Semantic Geometry of Latent Spaces

A well-trained latent space is not a random jumble of points; it has a meaningful structure, or a semantic geometry. The model organizes its conceptual map along intuitive axes, where different directions correspond to specific design transformations. Moving in one direction might transition a design from an "open" to an "enclosed" space, while moving in another could shift its style from classical to parametric.

This intelligent organization isn't programmed manually; it emerges as the AI learns the statistical patterns within massive architectural datasets. Empirical studies show that common architectural features form dense "clusters" or neighborhoods within the latent space. In contrast, the sparse, uncharted regions- the latent "frontier"- represent novel or unexplored design possibilities. Consequently, the latent space functions as a cognitive map of architectural potential, where traveling across it becomes an intentional act of design exploration.

## Navigating Latent Space: Mechanisms and Techniques

Navigating a latent space involves controlled movement through its high-dimensional geometry. Architects and designers can use several sophisticated techniques to guide this "latent space traversal":

- **Prompt Conditioning:** This technique uses text descriptions to guide the generative process. An architect can use a prompt like "a modernist glass structure at dusk" to steer the AI toward the region of the latent space that embodies those specific semantic and aesthetic qualities.
- **Cross-modal Retrieval:** To keep generated designs grounded and prevent unrealistic outputs, this method uses external data, such as real-world images or texts, to anchor the latent path in empirically rich zones of the conceptual map.
- **Latent Inversion:** This powerful editing technique works by "reverse-engineering" an existing design back to its latent vector. Once the core code is found, architects can manipulate it using intuitive adjustments, effectively editing the fundamental concept of the design.

- **Reinforcement Learning (RL)-guided Traversal:** This approach treats latent navigation as a goal-oriented task. An AI "agent" learns the most efficient paths through the latent space to satisfy specific design constraints or achieve desired architectural outcomes, such as optimizing for structural integrity or natural light.

These computational strategies place latent space navigation at the intersection of intuitive creativity and algorithmic precision, opening new frontiers for architectural innovation.

Chapter 6

# From Stone to Simulation

## The Evolution of Tools and Technologies in Architecture

Architecture, as both an art and a science, has always been a discipline defined by its tools. The technologies through which we conceive, represent, and realize buildings are never neutral instruments; they are active agents that shape the very boundaries of our imagination. The late theorist Marshall McLuhan's maxim that "the medium is the message" (McLuhan, 1964) resonates with particular force here. The evolution of architectural media—from the chisel to the computer—is a story not merely of increasing efficiency, but of profound shifts in epistemology, altering the fundamental modes of knowing through which architecture is understood and practiced.

The earliest architecture was born of direct, tactile engagement. The stone tools of prehistory determined the scale, form, and joinery of the first shelters, and knowledge was empirical, embodied, and inseparable from the act of making. The mind that designed the structure was the same hand that built it. A true separation between design and construction, between idea and object, was inconceivable.

This unity began to fracture in the Classical world. In ancient Egypt, Mesopotamia, Greece, and Rome, the introduction of geometry and proportional systems served as the first great tools of abstraction. The rope stretchers of the Nile Valley, who laid out temple foundations with astounding accuracy, and the compasses and straightedges of Greek geometers introduced not only precision but a profound conceptual division between the design and its execution. As Joseph Rykwert (1996) notes, this was the first epistemological divide between drawing and building, a moment when the architectural idea could be held and perfected as an abstract entity before a single stone was laid.

DOI: 10.1201/9781003637691-7

Throughout the medieval period, this division was partially reconciled in the figure of the master builder. In the great Gothic workshops, design, engineering, and construction knowledge were reintegrated into a single, authoritative role. The tools remained rudimentary—string, chalk, and treasured wooden templates—but the intellectual toolkit expanded dramatically, incorporating complex stereotomy, symbolic geometries, and daring structural experimentation (Bork, 2011). The cathedral's tracing floor, or *loge de trait*, emerged as a critical technology—a full-scale design surface where complex vaults and window traceries were worked out. It was a drawing, yes, but one that remained grounded in a 1:1 scale, a direct link between abstract geometry and the material logic of the building site.

The Renaissance, however, marked a complete and irreversible rupture. The invention of linear perspective by artists and architects like Brunelleschi and Alberti, coupled with the widespread availability of paper, allowed for the total externalization of spatial ideas. The architectural vision could now be captured, manipulated, and circulated, entirely detached from the constraints of physical construction (Panofsky, 1991). Leon Battista Alberti, in his seminal treatise *De re aedificatoria*, famously codified this new reality, defining the architect as a pure intellectual, distinct from the (now subordinate) builder. The architect's tools were no longer the hammer and chisel, but the drawing compass, the scale ruler, and the mind. Architecture had become a discipline of representational projection.

This trajectory toward abstraction and standardization accelerated through the subsequent centuries. The Enlightenment brought mechanical drawing devices and perspective machines that mirrored the era's obsession with rationality. The Industrial Revolution, with its new materials of iron and glass, demanded new calculative tools and methods of representation. Descriptive geometry, formalized by Gaspard Monge in the late 18th century, provided a rigorous mathematical system for projecting three-dimensional forms onto two-dimensional surfaces, establishing a direct lineage to modern digital modeling (Monge, 1798/2001).

Modernism, while embracing the aesthetic of the machine, also reconceived the architect as a systems thinker. As Antoine Picon (2010) has argued, the focus shifted toward optimization and information management. Tools like the planimeter and early structural calculators allowed architects to engage with space and performance quantitatively. The standardized, modular systems championed by architects like Le Corbusier (1923/2007) were, in essence, abstract algorithms for living, designed for mass replication.

It was against this backdrop that the true foundations of computational design were laid in the mid-20th century. In 1963, Ivan Sutherland's doctoral thesis introduced Sketchpad, a program that was nothing short of revolutionary. For the first time, a designer could interact directly with a graphical interface, manipulating digital shapes with a light pen (Sutherland, 1963). More importantly, Sketchpad introduced constraint-based design; it understood relationships, not just lines. This was the birth of parametric thinking.

Simultaneously, the intellectual currents of cybernetics and early artificial intelligence research began to flow into architectural discourse, most notably through figures like Nicholas Negroponte at the Architecture Machine Group at MIT (Negroponte, 1970; Mitchell, 1990). They envisioned a future where the computer would be more than a passive drafting tool; it would be an active collaborator, a co-designer. While this vision was far ahead of its time, it planted the seeds for the paradigm shift to come. By the 1970s and 1980s, the first commercial Computer-Aided Design (CAD) systems emerged, moving these experimental ideas into mainstream practice and marking the definitive epistemological watershed: the transition from a world of physical representation to one of computational abstraction had begun.

## Computer-Aided Design (CAD): History, Epistemology, and Impact

To the uninitiated, Computer-Aided Design (CAD) might appear merely as a technological enhancement—little more than a digital substitution for pencils, compasses, and paper. Such a simplistic interpretation, however, profoundly underestimates the deeper epistemological shift CAD has engendered. The advent of CAD in the second half of the twentieth century was not just about digitizing architectural drawings; it represented a fundamental transformation in how architecture is thought, conceptualized, and represented. Indeed, the history of CAD is more than a technical chronicle—it narrates the story of how representational technologies have reshaped architectural thinking itself, transitioning progressively from embodied craftsmanship, through abstract representation, and ultimately toward computational logic.

The conceptual foundations for CAD predate its practical realization by several decades. Already in the 1940s, visionary thinkers like Vannevar Bush were imagining computational devices that could augment human cognition. Bush's 1945 article, *As We May Think*, described the Memex—an imaginative, theoretical device enabling users to store and retrieve information in associative, non-linear ways (Bush, 1945). While not specifically conceived as a design tool, the Memex foreshadowed a future where information processing expanded human cognitive capacities, laying the philosophical groundwork for what would later become CAD.

By the late 1950s, digital computers were beginning to find practical application in engineering fields such as aerospace and automotive industries, primarily for numerical control machining tasks. Engineers soon recognized that these powerful machines could offer more than mere calculation—they held the promise of assisting in design representation and facilitating iterative modification.

However, the first true CAD system did not originate within architecture itself but rather emerged from the discipline of computer science. In 1963, Ivan Sutherland, as part of his Ph.D. research at MIT, developed Sketchpad, the first program that allowed direct graphical interaction with digital displays (Sutherland, 1963). Sketchpad enabled users to create geometric shapes, manipulate them directly using a revolutionary device called a "light pen," and apply constraints—such as ensuring that lines remained parallel or circles stayed tangent. This marked a radical shift, introducing the powerful concept of associative design logic: geometric forms ceased to be static graphical entities and instead became dynamic objects governed by mathematical and logical constraints. Sutherland's innovations anticipated by several decades the core principles of parametric and constraint-based modeling that would eventually become central to contemporary architectural practice. Indeed, Sketchpad's significance extended far beyond CAD itself, becoming foundational for computer graphics, interaction design, and even early conceptions of virtual reality.

Following Sketchpad's revolutionary insights, CAD development progressed rapidly, though initially not within architectural circles. Industries such as aerospace and automotive engineering became the early adopters, creating customized CAD systems suited to their highly specialized needs. Among these pioneering efforts was the DAC (Design Augmented by Computer) system developed at General Motors in the mid-1960s. Subsequently, aerospace corporations like McDonnell Douglas and Lockheed developed proprietary systems dedicated to aircraft design (Goodacre et al., 2012). These early systems were vector-based, providing unprecedented precision in representing lines and curves. Nevertheless, their enormous cost and reliance on large mainframe computers rendered them prohibitively expensive and technically complex, effectively excluding most architectural practitioners from accessing this emerging technology. Architecture thus remained conspicuously absent from the early CAD revolution—a gap that would persist until the more accessible technological environment of the 1980s (al-Rawi, 2020).

This technological landscape dramatically shifted in the early 1980s, shaped by two decisive developments: the rise of the personal computer and the advent of commercially available CAD software tailored explicitly for architects and designers. In 1982, Autodesk released AutoCAD, the first commercially successful CAD software explicitly designed for personal computers (Encarnação et al., 1990). Unlike previous mainframe-dependent systems, AutoCAD was affordable, adaptable, and accessible to the average architectural office, marking the democratization of CAD technology.

AutoCAD's interface embraced a two-dimensional vector-based drawing paradigm reminiscent of traditional drafting methods. This familiarity facilitated rapid adoption among architects but also inadvertently imposed significant constraints. Early CAD workflows remained conceptually anchored to analog-era logics, representing architecture as a collection of lines, curves, and flat geometric entities. Nonetheless, AutoCAD introduced a critical transformation in architectural practice: digital drawings were no longer physical artifacts but became dynamic datasets- modifiable, duplicable, and increasingly interoperable with other digital platforms.

Through these incremental yet profound shifts, CAD transitioned architecture from the tangible realm of analog craftsmanship into the intangible yet highly flexible digital domain, redefining not only representation but the epistemological foundations of architectural thought itself.

## The Rise of 3D CAD

The late 1980s and early 1990s marked a significant evolution in CAD technology- from two-dimensional drafting toward comprehensive three-dimensional modeling. Architectural software such as ArchiCAD, first introduced in 1987, and subsequently MicroStation and AutoCAD's own 3D capabilities, allowed architects, for the first time, to visualize, manipulate, and explore architectural forms directly within a three-dimensional digital environment (Kalay, 2004). This transition in CAD paralleled and indeed reinforced broader shifts occurring within architectural culture itself. Architectural thinking increasingly embraced volumetric and spatial reasoning, moving away from purely planar conceptions. Early experiments with complex and curvilinear geometries became feasible, stimulating architects to explore shapes previously constrained by manual drafting techniques. Concurrently, digital visualization became integral to the design presentation process, allowing architects to communicate complex spatial ideas more effectively to clients and stakeholders (Goodacre et al., 2012).

Despite this substantial technological advancement, the early 3D CAD tools remained predominantly representational, primarily depicting architectural forms rather than embedding deeper informational or parametric logic. They offered compelling visual simulations but lacked the parametric intelligence and richly embedded data structures that would characterize subsequent generations of software, particularly Building Information Modeling (BIM) systems.

The evolution from manual drawing toward CAD was more than a mere transition in representational medium; it signified a profound conceptual shift from mere representation toward active simulation. As William J. Mitchell articulated in his influential 1990 work, The Logic of Architecture, CAD fundamentally altered architectural epistemology by enabling architects to construct computational models that could be examined, interrogated, manipulated, and optimized in unprecedented ways. Architectural forms became computational entities—dynamic models that were no longer static depictions but active participants in the design process. Thus, the computer transitioned from a drafting instrument to a genuine design partner, a medium for computational reasoning and experimentation.

Moreover, CAD opened the door to integrating performance analysis into early-stage design thinking. Architects began incorporating structural, thermal, and environmental evaluations directly within their digital workflows, foreshadowing the comprehensive, information-centric design approach fully realized in BIM. Consequently, architectural knowledge increasingly became data-driven, with the design process extensively mediated through digital tools. By the late 1990s, CAD had become ubiquitous in architectural practice, transforming not only how architecture was represented but also fundamentally altering how architectural knowledge was generated, validated, and disseminated.

Indeed, the widespread adoption of CAD represented a critical epistemological threshold in architecture: design practice was now deeply entwined with digital mediation and data-centric methodologies. Architects found their roles evolving toward those of data orchestrators, responsible not only for form-making but also for managing complex information structures and computational workflows. As Mario Carpo later argued, the digital turn inaugurated by CAD set architecture on a trajectory toward algorithmic authorship, design automation, and computational creativity (Carpo, 2011).

## Building Information Modeling (BIM): From Representation to Integrated Knowledge Systems

If Computer-Aided Design (CAD) transformed the architectural drawing into a manipulable digital object, Building Information Modeling (BIM) took a more radical and philosophically profound step: it redefined architectural design as an ontologically rich, multi-dimensional data environment. While CAD remained tethered to geometry- focused on the representation of lines, surfaces, and volumes- BIM shifted the epistemic frame toward the modeling of information. It allowed architects not only to depict a building's form but to embed within that form the totality of its materiality, structural logic, energy performance, construction costs, lifecycle trajectory, and even post-occupancy behaviors. BIM, in this sense, did not merely add information to form; it restructured the very notion of what form is.

In philosophical terms, BIM signifies a movement from representational thinking to ontological modeling. The architect, no longer a draughtsman illustrating the appearance of a future object, assumes the role of a modeler of being. A BIM model is not just a likeness of a building; it is its digital twin- an entity with internal logics and attributes that correspond to real-world functions and behaviors. The drawing, once the final product of design intent, is now an extractable projection of an underlying, data-driven ontology.

The conceptual groundwork for this shift was laid decades earlier, in the 1960s and 1970s, by computing pioneers and architectural theorists who began imagining a future where buildings would be conceived not as collections of drawings but as structured digital models. Among these early visionaries was Charles Eastman, who in 1975 introduced the idea of Building Description Systems (BDS), one of the earliest proposals for object-based digital representations of buildings (Eastman, 1975). Around the same period, Nicholas Negroponte and the Architecture Machine Group at MIT were exploring the convergence of computing and design, developing theoretical frameworks and prototypical tools that anticipated many of the principles later embedded in BIM (Negroponte, 1970). While the practical application of these ideas was constrained by the technological limitations of the time, they offered a conceptual template for thinking about buildings as integrated systems of data and behavior rather than as static visual artifacts.

By the 1980s and early 1990s, the influence of these theoretical foundations began to take concrete shape. Commercial CAD platforms gradually introduced three-dimensional modeling and rudimentary object-based design elements. Graphisoft's ArchiCAD, launched in 1987, was among the first tools to allow architects to design not simply with lines and curves but with parametric objects- walls, doors, windows- each encoded with attributes and behaviors (Kalay, 2004). This marked a crucial epistemological transition: architectural drawing evolved from being a two-dimensional act of representation into a structured assembly of data-rich elements. A wall was no longer just a shape; it had thickness, material, thermal properties, and a defined relationship to adjacent components.

However, these early object-based systems still fell short of what would later be recognized as full-fledged BIM. While they introduced discrete parametric elements and enabled rudimentary coordination across design layers, they lacked the systemic integration of data necessary for true lifecycle modeling. BIM as we understand it today- capable of connecting design to construction, performance simulation, scheduling, cost analysis, and facility management- would only emerge with the maturation of software infrastructures and interoperability standards in the early twenty-first century.

What began as a speculative vision in the 1970s eventually matured into a dominant design paradigm, one that repositions architecture within the broader context of systems thinking and digital ecology. BIM not only redefined how architects work; it redefined what it means to design.

## The Emergence of BIM as a Paradigm

The emergence of Building Information Modeling (BIM) as a dominant paradigm in architectural practice began in the late 1990s and gained momentum through the early 2000s. Although the term "Building Information Modeling" was popularized by Jerry Laiserin in the early 2000s, Autodesk had already been using the phrase internally since the 1990s (Laiserin, 2002). This period marked a significant maturation in digital design, wherein multiple software platforms began offering fully integrated modeling environments that exceeded the limits of earlier CAD and object-based systems.

Among the key developments was the creation of Revit in 2000, a platform designed from the ground up to support parametric modeling and information integration. Autodesk acquired Revit in 2002, further accelerating its adoption. ArchiCAD, which had pioneered object-based design as early as 1987, continued to evolve in this period, expanding its capabilities to incorporate increasingly complex data layers. Bentley Systems, through its MicroStation platform and its BIM-oriented extensions, also entered the arena, offering multidisciplinary support for infrastructure and architectural projects.

Unlike earlier CAD tools, which focused on geometric representation, these new BIM platforms enabled a fundamentally different mode of design practice. Multi-disciplinary collaboration became structurally embedded within the software: architects, structural engineers, and mechanical, electrical, and plumbing (MEP) specialists could work simultaneously within the same model. Parametric control ensured that a single change- say, the movement of a wall or resizing of a window- automatically propagated across all related drawings, schedules, and quantities. Moreover, every element in the model was no longer a shape but a data container, holding information about material properties, energy performance, cost implications, and construction logistics.

This evolution marked the transformation of the model into a knowledge system: not merely a representational artifact but an operational repository of design, engineering, and building information. The implications of this transformation were not solely technical. BIM redefined the very ontology of architectural practice. As Mario Carpo (2011) and Antoine Picon (2010) have argued, the digital turn in architecture is part of a larger cultural reorientation toward algorithmic reasoning and data-driven epistemologies. BIM is a concrete manifestation of this shift. It treats the building not as a finished object to be depicted, but as a dynamic and evolving dataset. The architect's role, in this new framework, expands to include information management, system coordination, and predictive modeling, collapsing previously distinct phases of design, analysis, and even fabrication into a continuous digital process.

Perhaps most critically, BIM enables simulation rather than mere representation. With performance engines embedded into the design environment, architects are now able to simulate thermal conditions, structural behaviors, daylight distribution, and even human circulation patterns before a single component is physically constructed. This anticipatory capacity reconfigures the temporality of architectural knowledge: no longer retrospective or speculative, but predictive and operative.

By the 2010s, BIM had become the dominant standard for complex architectural and engineering projects in most industrialized nations, though its adoption varied globally. While regions like North America, Europe, and parts of Asia embraced BIM for large-scale construction, other markets continued to rely on traditional 2D CAD or hybrid workflows due to cost barriers, training gaps, or fragmented industry practices.

BIM's rise facilitated a shift toward more integrated project delivery methods, most notably Integrated Project Delivery (IPD), a collaborative framework where architects, engineers, contractors, and clients align their workflows around a shared model. However, while BIM enabled IPD, full implementation of IPD remained limited due to entrenched contractual norms. Instead, many projects adopted intermediate collaboration models (such as BIM Level 2 in the UK), where stakeholders exchanged data without fully restructuring their agreements.

Beyond design and construction, BIM expanded into lifecycle management, though its post-occupancy use was often inconsistent. In theory, BIM models could support facility management, energy monitoring, and renovations, effectively turning buildings into dynamically managed "digital twins." In practice, many models were underutilized after handover, as owners lacked the infrastructure or incentives to maintain them. Still, the potential for BIM to bridge design and long-term operations marked a significant evolution in architectural practice. Additionally, BIM's data-rich environment enabled advances in automation and prefabrication. Direct links between BIM models and fabrication technologies (such as CNC machinery and robotic assembly) allowed for precision manufacturing of building components. Yet these innovations were primarily applied to discrete systems (e.g., modular facades or MEP modules) rather than entire projects, as traditional construction methods still dominated the industry.

## Parametricism: From Variation to Algorithmic Design Intelligence

By the early 2000s, architecture stood poised for yet another conceptual and technical transformation. If the introduction of Computer-Aided Design (CAD) had marked the digitization of drawing, and if Building Information Modeling (BIM) had advanced that trajectory into integrated, information-rich systems, then parametricism signaled an even more radical departure. Parametric design proposed that architecture be conceived not as a fixed object, nor as a static assembly of parts, but as an algorithmic system- one governed by rules, parameters, and relationships. It reoriented the discipline from the representation of form to the orchestration of variability. In contrast to early dismissals of parametricism as merely an aesthetic trend defined by fluid surfaces or complex curves, its true significance lay in its epistemological break: it made design behavior-driven, systemic, and adaptive.

The conceptual roots of parametricism long predate the emergence of the term itself. Already in the 1960s, architectural theorists and computational visionaries began exploring how design might be systematized, programmed, and rendered responsive. At MIT, Nicholas Negroponte's Architecture Machine Group- established in 1967- articulated the provocative idea that computers could act not simply as passive drafting devices but as intelligent agents capable of collaborating with designers. These machines, he suggested, could operate within a bounded parameter space, proposing solutions based on evolving design criteria (Negroponte, 1970). Simultaneously in Britain, Cedric Price, Gordon Pask, and the larger cybernetic movement were developing concepts of adaptive architecture—buildings that could reconfigure themselves in real-time in response to changing environmental or social inputs (Price, 1971). The notion of design as an open system—responsive, contingent, and evolving—emerged here with striking clarity.

In parallel, figures like John Frazer pushed the frontier of computational architecture through the application of genetic algorithms and evolutionary logic. His work on the Autonomous House Project in the 1980s and 1990s used computational models not to represent preconceived forms but to *generate* forms through processes of selection, mutation, and emergence (Frazer, 1995). These early experiments cast design as a form of digital ecology, where the architect's role was not to sculpt form but to shape conditions under which form could evolve.

Yet for all their theoretical sophistication, these early efforts were constrained by the computational limitations of the time. Processing power, interface design, and software accessibility remained insufficient to operationalize these ideas on a large scale. It was not until the 1990s that two crucial shifts occurred. First, hardware and software capabilities grew exponentially, allowing even small studios to engage with complex modeling tasks. Second, a new generation of design tools emerged that embedded parametric logic into the architectural workflow.

Among the first to demonstrate this were Generative Components (GC), developed by Bentley Systems in the late 1990s. GC allowed designers to define relationships and rules among design elements such that modifying one component automatically propagated changes throughout the system- a rudimentary yet powerful manifestation of parametric dependency (Shelden, 2002). In parallel, general-purpose 3D software platforms such as Autodesk Maya and 3ds Max began to offer scripting environments, enabling designers to write procedural rules that could generate, transform, or animate geometric models.

The most influential development, however, came in the form of Grasshopper for Rhinoceros 3D, released in 2007. Created by David Rutten, Grasshopper offered a visual programming interface that allowed architects to compose algorithms by connecting visual nodes—each representing a geometric transformation, mathematical function, or logical operation—without needing to write code. This interface democratized access to parametric thinking. It placed algorithmic design within reach of architects who had little or no background in programming, allowing a generation of designers to experiment with complexity, emergence, and systemic variability.

While parametric design practices proliferated across the globe, the term *parametricism* itself was formally coined by Patrik Schumacher, principal of Zaha Hadid Architects, in a series of essays and manifestos beginning in the mid-2000s and culminating in landmark declarations in 2008 and 2010 (Schumacher, 2008; 2010). For Schumacher, parametricism was not merely a methodology or toolkit but an architectural style and cultural paradigm—one that succeeded modernism and postmodernism in historical continuity. He argued that the central task of contemporary architecture was to organize spatial complexity through continuous variation and responsiveness. Design elements, under this framework, were no longer treated as isolated objects but as variables within dynamic fields of interdependency. Architecture, Schumacher claimed, should embrace a logic of differentiation rather than repetition, responding in real time to social, environmental, and technological parameters.

This vision found built expression in the projects of Zaha Hadid Architects and several contemporaneous firms such as UNStudio, Future Systems, and Greg Lynn FORM. These practices leveraged the capacities of parametric tools to produce architectures of unprecedented formal and spatial complexity- buildings characterized by smooth gradients, non-linear transitions, and fluid topologies. Iconic projects such as the Heydar Aliyev Center in Baku, the MAXXI Museum in Rome, and the Yas Viceroy Hotel in Abu Dhabi embodied the ethos of parametricism not only in their appearance but in their underlying design processes. Geometry in these projects was not imposed but derived- emergent from fields of parameters, constraints, and algorithmic manipulations.

## Beyond Aesthetics: Parametricism as Process and Logic

Despite the widespread public attention given to the formal outcomes of parametric design- its smooth curves, fluid transitions, and visually striking geometries- the true significance of parametricism lies not in aesthetics, but in process and logic. It is a methodological revolution rather than a stylistic one. At its core, parametricism redefines the architectural design process as a field of relational modeling, algorithmic control, and iterative optimization. Architectural form, in this paradigm, is no longer a static object drawn in advance, but an emergent condition- generated through the dynamic interplay of variables, constraints, and computational logic.

Relational modeling becomes the foundational principle of this approach. Forms are not predefined; they arise from the relationships between elements. A wall, a window, or a structural truss is not placed arbitrarily or as an isolated component, but is generated through its parametric relationship to other parts of the system- sunlight, sightlines, structural loads, or circulation paths. Designers no longer manipulate forms directly; they manipulate the rules that govern them. In doing so, design shifts from a representational act to a systemic operation, where algorithms become the new medium of authorship.

The consequence of this shift is profound. Parametricism enables rapid iteration and performance-based exploration, facilitating a mode of practice where multiple design alternatives can be tested, compared, and optimized in near real-time. Traditional workflows, which relied on static sketches and manually revised drawings, give way to feedback-driven, data-intensive design loops. The computer no longer serves merely as a representational tool; it becomes an active collaborator in the generative process, capable of exploring vast solution spaces and surfacing configurations that might escape the intuition of the designer.

Moreover, parametric models are inherently extensible. They can be linked to environmental simulation tools, structural analysis engines, and fabrication protocols. A single parametric model can simultaneously respond to daylighting criteria, thermal performance, material optimization, and robotic fabrication constraints. This capacity for integration bridges previously siloed domains and supports design that is not only formally innovative but environmentally responsive and materially precise. Mass customization, once a contradiction in terms, becomes feasible through the parametrically-driven control of digital fabrication.

Yet as with any paradigm shift, parametricism has not been without its critics. Some have argued that the method's openness to formal complexity often resulted in gratuitous design—where visual spectacle overtook functional clarity. Others have pointed to the growing dependence on specific software ecosystems, which can create barriers for smaller firms or non-Western practitioners, exacerbating inequalities within the field. Perhaps most ironically, despite its emphasis on differentiation, parametricism has sometimes produced a recognizable and homogenous visual language—an aesthetic of smooth surfaces, blobby geometries, and continuous curves that, to some, felt more like a signature than a system.

However, such critiques often stem from misapplications or superficial appropriations of parametric tools, rather than inherent flaws in the methodology itself. When used rigorously, parametricism is not an aesthetic but a process—one that prioritizes adaptability, responsiveness, and the intelligent structuring of complexity. It is not about making forms look "parametric," but about ensuring that forms are the outcome of embedded reasoning and environmental intelligence.

By the 2010s, parametricism had evolved from an avant-garde experiment into a mainstream mode of design. Its principles found application far beyond the museum or cultural center. In urban design, parametric tools were deployed to simulate pedestrian flows, optimize sunlight exposure, and analyze urban morphology. In environmental architecture, designers used parametric models to integrate real-time feedback on daylighting, thermal comfort, and acoustic performance. In fabrication, parametric workflows drove the mass production of customized components, interfacing directly with CNC machines, robotic arms, and additive manufacturing technologies.

Crucially, parametricism laid the intellectual and technical foundation for the next generation of computational design. Out of its logic emerged new forms of generativity: machine learning-assisted modeling, evolutionary algorithms, and artificial intelligence-driven design systems. Grasshopper, the visual programming environment that had catalyzed parametricism's ascent, expanded into a rich ecosystem of plugins—Kangaroo for physics-based simulation, Ladybug for environmental analysis, Galapagos for genetic optimization, and, more recently, integration frameworks for neural networks and AI agents. What began as a rule-based modeling environment became a platform for integrating perception, simulation, and prediction.

The influence of parametric thinking has extended well beyond architecture. Its procedural logic has been adopted in industrial design, automotive engineering, aerospace, and even bio-design. From the shape of ergonomic chairs to the aerodynamic bodies of vehicles and the generative forms of tissue scaffolds, parametric logic has permeated disciplines that require the synthesis of form, function, and variability. This is the true legacy of parametricism: not an aesthetic legacy, but a methodological one. It has redefined how we think about design in the age of computation- not as the projection of static visions, but as the cultivation of systems capable of responding, evolving, and learning (Carpo, 2024).

## Architectural Intelligence: AI Architectures and Their Role in Design Thinking and Practice

As the architectural discipline enters what may prove to be its most consequential technological shift since the digitization of drawing, artificial intelligence (AI) has transitioned from an experimental curiosity to a central influence in architectural thought and practice. Yet, despite the ubiquity of "AI" in discourse, its deeper epistemological and operational implications for architecture remain under-examined. This chapter moves beyond surface-level enthusiasm or skepticism to interrogate the structural relationship between AI's computational architectures and the evolving epistemology of design.

The integration of AI into architectural workflows signals not just new tools but a paradigmatic shift in problem-solving, creativity, and conceptualization. From neural networks to generative models, AI is reshaping architectural imagination—not merely through novel outputs, but through fundamentally different logics of cognition and perception. Since the mid-2010s, machine learning (ML) has altered how architectural problems are formulated. Unlike rule-based parametric systems, where designers define explicit relationships, ML operates inductively, extracting patterns from data. Here, the architect no longer prescribes machine behavior but engages with systems that infer latent possibilities-shifting design from a descriptive practice (governed by predefined procedures) to a predictive-generative one (guided by learned correlations).

Central to this shift is the artificial neural network (ANN), as mentioned earlier, a computational structure loosely inspired by biological neurons. Early architectural applications focused on prediction—energy modeling, structural analysis, and occupant behavior—using ANNs' ability to discern nonlinear relationships beyond conventional algorithms. Crucially, these systems learned rather than followed scripts, adjusting their parameters through training data. This marked a transition from modeling architecture (as a fixed object) to learning architecture (as an emergent pattern from data) (Xu et al., 2020).

The advent of convolutional neural networks (CNNs) expanded AI's role from analysis to spatial cognition. By hierarchically processing visual data—from edges to complex forms—CNNs enabled style classification, urban morphology studies, and typological recognition at scales surpassing human capacity. This was not mere automation but an expansion of architectural perception, allowing designers to interrogate spatial datasets with unprecedented granularity.

More transformative was CNNs' shift toward generation. By the late 2010s, neural networks were not just analyzing but proposing forms, closing the loop between observation and creation (Ang et al., 2022). Here, AI began to act as a co-ideator, synthesizing solutions rather than executing instructions.

Generative adversarial networks (GANs) introduced a dialectical approach: a generator proposed designs, while a discriminator critiqued them, refining outputs through adversarial feedback. Architects adopted GANs for speculative façades, urban configurations, and housing typologies, where design became less about direct control and more about curating emergent possibilities (El Moussaoui, 2025a; Albukhari, 2025). Authorship grew distributed, with the architect steering processes rather than dictating forms (El Moussaoui, 2025c).

The most recent evolution, diffusion models, replaced adversarial training with probabilistic iteration, generating images by refining noise into coherent outputs. Tools like Midjourney and DALL·E allowed designers to prompt spatial proposals linguistically, yielding unexpected materialities and atmospheres.

## Autoencoders: Learning to Compress and Reconstruct Spatial Information

While much of the recent discourse surrounding Artificial Intelligence in architecture has concentrated on generative models such as GANs and diffusion systems, another class of neural architectures—autoencoders—has operated more quietly yet no less significantly in the background. Despite their relative lack of visibility in mainstream architectural AI narratives, autoencoders have served as foundational infrastructures for a wide range of experimental tools, research frameworks, and computational workflows.

At their core, autoencoders are composed of two neural components: an encoder that compresses high-dimensional input data into a lower-dimensional latent representation, and a decoder that reconstructs the original data from this compressed form. Unlike traditional compression algorithms, which apply predefined heuristics, autoencoders *learn* what features of the data are essential—what must be retained to meaningfully reconstruct the original—and what can be discarded without significant loss. This data-driven dimensionality reduction makes autoencoders particularly powerful in contexts where the underlying structure of the data is complex, abstract, or poorly defined.

Autoencoders have found application in several architectural contexts, particularly in typological synthesis. By learning compressed representations of architectural forms autoencoders can be used to generate new variations that interpolate across the learned design space. The latent vector, in this context, becomes not merely a compressed description but a generative axis- a space through which architects can explore alternative configurations that retain core features while opening up novel formal possibilities.

Beyond generative synthesis, autoencoders also support optimization and search. Their compressed latent spaces offer a significantly reduced design solution space, making it more computationally feasible to perform multi-objective optimization, especially when coupled with evolutionary algorithms or reinforcement learning frameworks. Instead of navigating the infinite complexities of a pixel-based or geometric design space, designers can operate within a learned space that preserves the architectural essence of the problem while allowing for efficient traversal and goal-seeking.

Another important application lies in image-to-image translation tasks. Autoencoders have been employed to map between different visual or spatial domains, for instance, in translating a neoclassical façade into a modernist interpretation, or simulating the adaptive reuse of an industrial structure into a civic building. In these applications, the encoder-decoder structure serves not only to reconstruct but to reinterpret, bridging stylistic or functional regimes in ways that human designers can guide but do not have to micromanage.

A particularly influential extension of this architecture is the Variational Autoencoder (VAE), which introduces stochasticity into the latent space. Rather than mapping inputs to fixed latent points, VAEs map them to probability distributions, enabling the generation of outputs that are both diverse and statistically coherent. This has proven especially useful in experimental design workflows where the goal is not to generate exact replicas but to explore formal and typological variations that remain within a learned envelope of plausibility. Unlike GANs, which rely on adversarial dynamics and often lack interpretability, VAEs offer a controlled and mathematically grounded space for design exploration—balancing novelty with intelligibility.

More recently, the logic of autoencoders has been integrated into the architecture of diffusion models, particularly in the form of latent diffusion. Here, the generative process is not performed directly in pixel space but in a compressed latent space learned by an autoencoder. This innovation, pioneered in models such as Stable Diffusion, has dramatically improved the computational efficiency of image generation and increased the fidelity of the results (Rombach et al., 2022). By shifting the generative task to a lower-dimensional yet semantically rich domain, latent diffusion reduces the noise and computational cost traditionally associated with high-resolution visual synthesis.

## Language as Design Interface: Large Language Models and Multimodal Reasoning

The advent of Large Language Models (LLMs), driven predominantly by transformer architectures, has expanded artificial intelligence's role in architecture far beyond visual recognition or data analysis, profoundly reshaping the conceptual reasoning processes underpinning design itself. Architects have begun to integrate LLMs not only into tasks involving textual content, such as project descriptions or script generation, but also into deeper processes of articulating design logic and intent. Platforms like ChatGPT, GPT-4o, and specialized domain-specific language models have become increasingly used for experimental workflows, enabling architects to translate plain-language descriptions into parametric code, generate design briefs, conduct preliminary feasibility analyses, summarize complex site conditions, and facilitate collaborative design conversations. Domain-specific LLMs are rare, but tools like Finch (for parametric design) demonstrate potential.

Moreover, as LLMs evolve into multimodal reasoning systems - capable of integrating text, imagery, and increasingly sophisticated spatial data- language emerges as a powerful new interface linking human intention with computational execution. This multimodal capacity fundamentally redefines the epistemology of design communication. Architects are no longer limited by purely visual or numeric forms of representation; instead, they can engage with AI systems through natural semantic reasoning, employing language to communicate nuanced, context-rich design intentions. In doing so, the traditional boundaries between linguistic, numeric, and spatial cognition are increasingly blurred, positioning language as a central mediator in the dialogue between human designers and AI collaborators (Burry and Burry, 2021).

Simultaneously, a related frontier—Spatial AI—is beginning to reshape architectural design through the development of systems capable not merely of processing spatial data, but actively reasoning about space. Emerging technologies such as spatially aware LLM prototypes, Neural Radiance Fields (NeRFs), and Graph Neural Networks (GNNs) exemplify this shift, pointing toward a future where AI participates directly in spatial cognition. For instance, SpatialGPT introduces conversational design workflows, enabling architects to articulate spatial goals and receive contextually sensitive, AI-generated design proposals. NeRFs allow rapid reconstruction of physical spaces into digital, manipulable three-dimensional models, greatly enhancing tasks such as design visualization, spatial experimentation, and heritage documentation. GNNs provide powerful mechanisms for understanding and generating spatial relationships, whether in building programs, structural systems, or urban networks. Collectively, these technologies challenge traditional distinctions between analysis and synthesis, hinting at a future of co-design environments in which human and machine cognition collaborate seamlessly, jointly shaping spatial outcomes.

Within this evolving landscape, Graph Neural Networks (GNNs) and three-dimensional transformer architectures represent two particularly promising classes of AI that deserve closer attention due to their potential to transform architectural reasoning fundamentally. Graph Neural Networks differ significantly from familiar architectures like Convolutional Neural Networks (CNNs), which are optimized primarily for grid-like, Euclidean data structures such as images. In contrast, GNNs excel at processing non-Euclidean, graph-structured data—precisely the types of data inherent to architectural and urban design. Rather than relying solely on geometric proximity, GNNs can directly analyze complex relational structures among spaces, components, and networks. Their application extends from optimizing adjacency in building programs and circulation flows to analyzing structural load paths and urban spatial networks, enabling architects to treat spatial topology not merely as geometric form but as computationally actionable logic (Bronstein et al., 2017).

At the same time, 3D transformers- extensions of transformer architectures that initially emerged in natural language processing-are now being adapted to interpret and manipulate complex three-dimensional spatial data. Models like PointNet++ and the latest generation of 3D vision transformers allow AI to parse point clouds, volumetric datasets, and complex spatial environments with remarkable precision (Qi et al., 2017; Zeng et al., 2023). These systems facilitate automation in previously challenging tasks such as automatic floor plan generation, urban morphological analysis, and adaptive spatial planning, signaling a shift towards computational systems capable not only of visualizing but also reasoning spatially in three dimensions.

Together, the emergence of LLMs as multimodal design interfaces and the growing sophistication of Spatial AI—particularly GNNs and 3D transformers—represent a profound evolution in architectural intelligence. Rather than merely automating or accelerating existing practices, these systems alter the epistemological foundations of architecture itself, enabling machines to engage in increasingly human-like spatial reasoning. Architects, therefore, find themselves not merely guiding passive computational tools, but engaging with active computational partners capable of understanding, interpreting, and shaping complex spatial ideas. This evolution foreshadows an architectural practice defined by continuous human-machine dialogue, collaboratively exploring and expanding the possibilities inherent in spatial design.

# Chapter 7

# AI Tools in Architectural Practice

## From Automation to Epistemic Partnership

As we have discussed, in the past two decades have witnessed an unprecedented acceleration in the development and adoption of AI tools across all disciplines. In architecture, however, this shift is not simply technological- it is epistemological. As AI systems transition from automating isolated tasks to influencing design logic itself, architects are facing not only new efficiencies but a redefinition of their role as designers, decision-makers, and, increasingly, as curators of computational thought.

This chapter examines the new generation of AI platforms now transforming architectural practice (Table 2). Rather than offering a catalog of software products, we will trace how these tools embody different AI methodologies- from data-driven analysis to generative synthesis- and how they are restructuring the architectural design process from pre-design to construction and even into post-occupancy. In Table 1 we see the architectural process, then we will see at each stage how did AI infiltrate the process.

By mapping these tool, we can understand them not merely as labor-saving devices but as operationalized intelligences that co-shape design thinking (El Moussaoui, 2025b).

DOI: 10.1201/9781003637691-8

**Table 1.** A table of the architecture phases from predesign to post-occupancy evaluation.

| Stage | Work |
|---|---|
| Pre-design/programming: | Client consultation and establishment of project goals, scope, and budget Professionals involved: Client, Architect, Interior Designer, and other consultants as needed |
| Site analysis: | Evaluation of the site's opportunities, constraints, and context Professionals involved: Architect, Landscape Architect, Civil Engineer, Environmental Consultant, and other specialists as needed |
| Schematic design (SD): | Creation of initial design concepts, sketches, and preliminary space planning Professionals involved: Architect, Interior Designer, Landscape Architect, Structural Engineer, Mechanical, Electrical, and Plumbing (MEP) Engineers, and other consultants as needed |
| Design development (DD): | Further development of the design, refining spatial relationships, materials, and finishes Professionals involved: Architect, Interior Designer, Landscape Architect, Structural Engineer, MEP Engineers, and other consultants as needed |
| Construction documents (CD): | Preparation of detailed drawings and specifications, which will be used for construction bidding, permitting, and construction Professionals involved: Architect, Interior Designer, Landscape Architect, Structural Engineer, MEP Engineers, and other consultants as needed |
| Permitting: | Submission of CDs to local authorities for review and approval Professionals involved: Architect, General Contractor, and possibly a Permit Expeditor |
| Construction administration (CA): | Oversight of construction, ensuring work is completed according to the CDs Professionals involved: Architect, Client, General Contractor, Subcontractors, and possibly a Construction Manager or Owner's Representative |
| Construction: | Execution of the actual building process, including site preparation, foundation work, building erection, and installation of systems Professionals involved: General Contractors, Subcontractors, and Trade Workers |
| Inspection and closeout: | Final inspections, punch list, and completion of any remaining work Professionals involved: Architect, Client, General Contractor, Building Inspectors, and possibly a Construction Manager or Owner's Representative |
| Post-occupancy evaluation (POE): | Assessment of the building's performance, user satisfaction, and identification of any issues to be addressed Professionals involved: Architect, Client, Building Occupants, and possibly a Post-Occupancy Evaluation Consultant |

## Pre-Design and Programming: AI as Contextual Analyst and Generator

The earliest stages of the architectural process- site analysis, feasibility studies, and program definition—have traditionally required labor-intensive data gathering and expert interpretation. AI has fundamentally disrupted this paradigm, automating not only the collection but the synthesis and interpretation of vast, multimodal datasets. The role of the architect is evolving from a data gatherer to a strategic interrogator of AI-driven insights.

Platforms such as Archistar.ai and Canoa exemplify this shift by algorithmically parsing complex, text-based municipal codes, geospatial data, and property records to generate sophisticated feasibility studies in minutes. They can instantly delineate permissible building envelopes, calculate maximum floor area ratios (FAR), and identify potential zoning conflicts. Beyond raw regulation, tools like Autodesk Forma and Digital Blue Foam integrate dynamic environmental analysis. They simulate hyperlocal conditions—solar exposure, wind turbulence, acoustic profiles, and thermal comfort—providing a quantitative basis for massing and orientation before a single line is drawn.

Furthermore, the advent of Large Language Models (LLMs) has introduced a qualitative dimension to this analysis. Custom-trained models can analyze community feedback, summarize demographic trends, and even assist in drafting the architectural program itself by identifying underserved local needs or proposing novel programmatic combinations based on precedent analysis. In this context, AI acts not merely as a faster calculator but as a contextual intelligence. It bridges raw data with design criteria, revealing non-obvious relationships—such as the correlation between local traffic patterns and optimal retail placement—and generating a data-rich foundation that becomes the strategic brief for the creative work to follow.

## Concept Generation and Early Design: AI as Creative Collaborator

Emerging from the data-driven landscape of the pre-design phase, the conceptual stage leverages AI not for analysis, but for synthesis and unfettered imagination. The quantitative constraints and opportunities identified by tools like Autodesk Forma become the implicit or explicit prompts for a new class of creative AI collaborators. This domain has seen the explosive adoption of text-to-image and image-to-image generative models, powered by diffusion algorithms and Generative Adversarial Networks (GANs).

Platforms such as Midjourney, DALL-E 3, and open-source interfaces like COMFY UI for Stable Diffusion have revolutionized architectural visualization. They operate in the language of semantics and aesthetics, allowing architects to translate abstract design intentions—"a brutalist library with soaring lightwells and warm timber accents"—into evocative, high-resolution imagery. These systems function not as deterministic rendering engines but as probabilistic co-creators, offering unexpected variations that can extend, challenge, or radically transform the designer's original vision. They allow for the exploration of mood, materiality, and form at a speed that is divorced from the labor of geometric modeling.

This visual exploration is complemented by tools like Finch3D and Hypar.ai, which integrate generative design with parametric logic. Here, the architect defines goals and constraints—spatial adjacencies, structural grids, efficiency targets—and the AI generates a vast solution space of viable design options. This moves beyond the 2D image to explore the fundamental logic of the building itself. The most advanced workflows now create a feedback loop, using tools like Kaedim , ComfyUI or Luma AI to translate a compelling 2D image generated by Midjourney into a preliminary 3D mesh, providing a tangible starting point for the more rigorous development that lies ahead. This phase, therefore, is about rapidly generating and visually testing a multitude of design hypotheses, setting the stage for their refinement and rationalization.

## Schematic and Design Development: From Representation to Simulation

The transition from conceptual ideation to Schematic Design (SD) and Design Development (DD) does not signify an abandonment of generative AI, but rather a strategic reframing of its application. These phases are characterized by a productive ambiguity; while core design questions of massing, circulation, and program are being resolved, the specific geometric and material expressions remain fluid. It is precisely this intermediate state—less constrained than construction documentation but more defined than a pure concept—that creates a fertile ground for a new class of AI tools.

While the initial concept phase thrives on the unconstrained, probabilistic nature of text-to-image models, SD and DD benefit immensely from more guided generative techniques. This is where the initial, often chaotic, creativity of tools like Midjourney and Stable Diffusion is harnessed and disciplined. Using powerful extensions such as ControlNet (which we will learn how to use in the coming chapters with

ComfyUI), architects can now feed these diffusion models with specific geometric inputs—a simple massing model from SketchUp, a floor plan sketch from Rhino, or even a section diagram. The AI then uses this input not as a mere suggestion but as a structural scaffold, generating high-fidelity architectural visualizations that adhere to the specified spatial logic while exploring myriad possibilities for materiality, fenestration, and atmospheric quality. This workflow, integrated directly into design environments through plugins like Veras for Revit, LookX for SketchUp, and Swapp for Rhino, allows for the rapid testing of facade compositions or interior lighting schemes in minutes, a task that would have traditionally required hours of manual modeling and rendering. The "imprecision" of the AI becomes a feature, suggesting novel details and textures that can inform the ongoing design process without the computational overhead of a fully detailed Building Information Model (BIM).

Concurrently, another category of AI tools operationalizes the project's constraints, moving from representation to intelligent generation of form and layout. Platforms such as Autodesk Forma (formerly Spacemaker) use generative algorithms to analyze a site and produce dozens of massing options optimized for environmental factors like solar radiation, wind patterns, and noise pollution, providing quantitative feedback in real-time. Similarly, tools like Testfit.io and Architechtures.ai focus on programmatic resolution, automating the creation of code-compliant and highly efficient building layouts—from apartment units to parking garages—within a given building envelope. These systems do not merely arrange spaces; they understand and apply complex rule sets, liberating the architect from the tedious aspects of feasibility studies and allowing them to focus on higher-level strategic decisions.

The true power of AI in these intermediate phases lies in the establishment of a rapid, iterative feedback loop between these different modalities. A massing strategy developed in Autodesk Forma can be exported to Revit, where its interior is rationalized by Testfit. A key section of this rationalized model can then be visualized with Veras to study its aesthetic and atmospheric potential. The performance of this refined design can then be analyzed by simulation platforms like Cove.tool or Hypar.ai, which use machine learning to predict energy use, daylight autonomy, and construction costs. The data from this analysis feeds back into the next iteration, creating a dynamic dialogue between qualitative intent and quantitative performance. In this way, AI transforms SD and DD from a linear sequence of drawings into a holistic, multi-modal process, radically accelerating the architect's ability to explore, validate, and refine design hypotheses with unprecedented speed and intelligence.

## Construction Documentation: AI and the Automation of Precision

Following the iterative refinement and data-validated decisions of the Design Development phase, the project transitions into the production of construction documents (CDs)—a stage historically defined by meticulous, repetitive, and time-consuming labor. Here, AI's role pivots from creative exploration and optimization to the automation of precision. The detailed Building Information Model (BIM), now enriched with performance data and design intent from previous phases, becomes the direct input for a new generation of AI-powered documentation tools.

Platforms like Swapp.ai, Blueprints AI, and the automation features within BricsCAD BIM are at the forefront of this shift. Trained on vast libraries of completed projects, industry standards (such as the Architectural Graphic Standards), and best-practice construction details, these AI systems function as expert "co-pilots" for BIM technicians. They can automate the generation of entire drawing sets, taking a 3D wall or roof assembly from the model and automatically creating the necessary plan, section, and detail drawings, complete with standardized annotations, dimensions, and material tags. This process dramatically reduces manual drafting time and, more importantly, minimizes the risk of human error and inconsistencies across a large document set.

Crucially, this is more than mere automation. Through sophisticated pattern recognition, these tools perform semantic checks that go beyond simple geometric clash detection. An AI can identify a specified window detail that is incompatible with the wall's fire rating, flag inconsistencies between the door schedule and the hardware specifications, or even suggest more efficient material cuts based on standard stock sizes. By embedding this layer of predictive quality control directly into the documentation workflow, AI not only accelerates the production of CDs but also enhances their accuracy and constructability, delivering a highly reliable and internally consistent digital twin that is primed for fabrication and construction.

## Construction Sequencing and Lifecycle Management: Toward Autonomous Building Processes

The meticulously detailed and error-checked digital twin produced during the documentation phase becomes the foundational dataset for the next frontier: AI-driven construction and logistics. This is where design intelligence translates directly into the act of making. Tools such as ALICE Technologies and nPlan ingest the complete BIM and apply generative algorithms and reinforcement learning to simulate and de-risk the entire construction process. By playing out millions of potential construction timelines—factoring in complex dependencies, supply chain logistics, labor availability, and even predictive weather data—these platforms identify optimal, cost-effective pathways for project delivery, transforming the Gantt chart from a static document into a dynamic, intelligent strategy.

This intelligence extends from scheduling to the physical site. AI-powered 4D and 5D BIM simulations visualize the construction sequence over time and link it to cost, while computer vision systems monitor site progress, automatically verifying that work completed matches the digital plan and flagging deviations in real-time. This creates a cyber-physical feedback loop. Furthermore, we are witnessing the rise of robotic construction applications that close the gap between digital instruction and physical execution. Systems like Canvas (for robotic drywall finishing), Hadrian X (for robotic bricklaying), and various forms of robotic prefabrication translate the digital twin's data directly into precise physical actions. Although still maturing, these developments point toward a new paradigm of architectural production—a digital master builder model where design intent is preserved with unparalleled fidelity from concept to execution.

## Post-Occupancy Evaluation and Adaptive Design Intelligence

The building's lifecycle does not conclude with its construction; rather, it enters a new phase of continuous dialogue with its users and environment, facilitated by its living digital twin. The model, born in design and validated in construction, now becomes an active repository for post-occupancy data, collected via a network of IoT (Internet of Things) sensors monitoring everything from energy consumption and air quality to occupancy patterns and circulation flows.

This is where advanced machine learning models, such as graph neural networks (GNNs), provide profound insights. By conceptualizing the building as a complex network of interconnected spaces, systems, and users, GNNs can analyze relational data to identify inefficient circulation paths, predict equipment maintenance needs before failure occurs, and recommend operational adjustments to enhance user comfort and reduce energy waste. The Digital Twin—this dynamic, data-rich replica of the built environment—embodies this post-occupancy intelligence. (El Moussaoui, 2025b).

**Table 2.** A review of AI applications that could be used at various phases in architecture.

| **Stage** | **AI tool** | **Application in Architecture** | **Process** |
|---|---|---|---|
| Pre-Design/ Programming | Varys<br>Midjourney<br>DALL-E 2/3<br>Chatmind<br>Adobe Firefly<br>Maket<br>Architechtures<br>Designs.ai<br>COMFY UI | Analyze and optimize space relationships and usage | Manual gathering of project requirements and programming |
| Analysis | XKool Testfit<br>Autodesk Forma<br>Digital Blue Foam<br>Sidewalk Labs<br>Civils.ai<br>Archistar.ai<br>Finch3d<br>Visualise.ai<br>Autodesk<br>Generative Design<br>Interiorai<br>ArchitecHtures<br>RoomGPT<br>Photoshop (Beta)<br>Cove.tool<br>ReRoom.ai<br>SmartDrew<br>Programa<br>HomeByMe<br>Hutch<br>IKEA Place<br>LexSet<br>ReRender.ai<br>ARK<br>Sloyd<br>ArkoAI<br>RoomGPT<br>ToTree<br>Collovgpt<br>Hestyaai<br>ReimagineHome<br>Homedesignai<br>PromeAI<br>Homestyler<br>Spoak<br>Spacely<br>Fulhaus Ludwig<br>Veras<br>Fabrie<br>Mnml.ai<br>Lookx<br>Getfoorplan<br>Runway.ai | Process and analyze geographical and environmental data<br>Concept generation and design exploration using GANs<br>Create images and renders from text descriptions or sketch models<br>Generating plans | Site analysis, including studying geographical, environmental, and contextual factors<br>Sketches, physical models, and design exploration |

*Table 2 contd. ...*

***...Table 2 contd.***

| **Stage** | **AI tool** | **Application in Architecture** | **Process** |
|---|---|---|---|
| Design Development | Autodesk's Dreamcatcher<br>LLMs (ChatGPT, Gemini, etc.)<br>Finch3d<br>LEO<br>Hypar.ai<br>nTopology | Automate design exploration and optimization processes | Material Selection and Detailing |
| Construction Documents | Blueprints AI<br>BricsCAD<br>Kreo | BIM automation: design, cost estimation, and construction planning | Preparation of CDs, including drawings and specifications |

# Chapter 8

# A Framework for Critical AI Practice
## Ethics, Authorship, and the New Architectural Agency

The preceding chapters have charted a course through the theoretical landscape of a discipline in the throes of a paradigm shift. We have traced the long history of our tools—from the compass and rule to the complex algorithms of parametric design—placing our current moment within a broader technological lineage. We have deconstructed the architectures of artificial intelligence, peeling back the layers of neural networks and diffusion models to reveal the statistical logic that animates them. In doing so, we have established a critical framework for navigating the profound ethical and creative questions they pose. The central argument has been this: AI is not merely a new instrument for accelerated efficiency, but a cognitive and operative force that is fundamentally reshaping the epistemological foundations of architecture. It is altering how we know by introducing probabilistic, data-driven insights alongside empirical analysis; how we see by granting us access to the latent visual possibilities embedded within vast datasets; and how we create by shifting the locus of design from direct manipulation to the orchestration of complex generative systems (El Moussaoui, 2025b). Now, with this theoretical groundwork firmly laid, we pivot from the abstract to the applied, from the "why" to the "how." This section of the book is conceived as a workshop, a technical manual and strategic guide for the architect who seeks not just to use AI, but to engage with it, to challenge it, and ultimately, to master it as a medium.

A passive, uncritical reliance on generative tools constitutes one of the most significant professional risks for the contemporary architect. Left to

DOI: 10.1201/9781003637691-9

their own devices, these systems exhibit a powerful tendency to regress toward the mean—an algorithmic inclination to endlessly recombine the most statistically prevalent patterns within their training data. The result is a frictionless, predictable, and ultimately homogenous aesthetic (El Moussaoui, 2025b). Uncontrolled AI outputs are the architectural embodiment of this smoothness: they produce forms that are visually plausible and immediately consumable, yet are devoid of the very friction, specificity, and deep contextual reasoning that give architecture its soul and purpose. The "friction" in architecture arises from the stubborn particularities of a site, the complex needs of a community, the inherent limitations of a material, the critical dialogue with history. An architecture of smoothness ignores this, offering a generic solution that is placeless, timeless, and therefore, meaningless.

To avoid this existential trap—to prevent our practice from devolving into a superficial exercise in aesthetic recombination—we must learn to actively control the machine, otherwise we wont be capable to leverage our creativity with the machine's aid (Fig. 2). The goal of this practical guide is to provide you with the technical grammar and strategic syntax to do precisely that. We will move beyond the opaque "black box" of simple text-to-image prompting and into the open-source modular environment of ComfyUI. Here, the generative process is not a single command but a visual algorithm, a design pipeline where every parameter can be isolated, interrogated, and directed. You will learn to construct bespoke workflows that embed your specific design intent at every stage. We will translate your architectural knowledge into direct visual guides using control models that compel the AI to respect geometric and spatial logic. We will leverage curated data inputs to bias the system toward context-

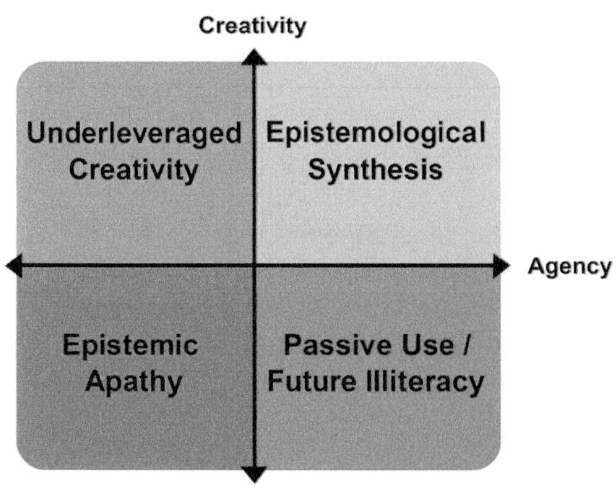


**Figure 2.** Epistemological Conditions of AI-Driven Design: A quadrant model mapping the intersection of creativity and agency. The horizontal axis represents the degree of agency (from low to high).

aware solutions, and we will build iterative feedback loops that enable a true dialogue between designer and machine. Additionally, we will learn how to prompt properly to have the best outcome with all the variable parameters available on Midjourney. This is a fundamental shift in practice from prompting to programming, from making a request to designing a system. Crucially, this is not about suppressing the machine's creative "hallucination," but about learning to architect it. Mastery lies not in stifling the stochastic engine of the AI, but in carefully constructing the boundaries and constraints within which it can productively dream, ensuring its outputs are not a regression to the mean, but an exploration of profound, meaningful, and truly architectural possibilities.

## The Politics and Ethics of Data: Curating the Architectural Imagination

Central to this critical engagement with artificial intelligence is the foundational understanding that datasets—the vast digital archives from which AI learns—are never neutral. They are ideological and cultural artifacts, laden with the implicit biases, historical exclusions, and hegemonic assumptions of the societies that created them (El Moussaoui, 2025d). The standard, web-scraped dataset, for example, vastly over-represents Western, modernist, and high-capital architectural production, while systematically under-representing vernacular, indigenous, and non-Western traditions. Consequently, an AI trained on this skewed digital diet inherits and perpetuates these biases, equating "architecture" with a narrow, canonical set of styles. This realization places a profound ethical and political responsibility upon the architect: to move from being a passive consumer of AI outputs to an active curator of its inputs. The act of consciously selecting, augmenting, and challenging datasets—for instance, by building custom archives of local vernacular traditions or by fine-tuning models on the works of historically marginalized designers—is not a mere technical preliminary. It is a crucial act of injecting epistemological diversity and critical resistance into the generative process. By curating the machine's sources of knowledge, the architect can proactively counteract dominant aesthetic regimes, broaden the AI's imaginative scope, and steer its creative potential toward more equitable, inclusive, and culturally specific architectural futures.

## Redefining Architectural Authorship in the AI Era

The integration of artificial intelligence into design practice fundamentally challenges and redefines traditional conceptions of architectural authorship. The dominant model of the last century, epitomized by the "starchitect" phenomenon, has been overwhelmingly individualistic, autographic, and ocular-centric-privileging the singular vision of a master architect whose unique "eye" and "hand" dictate the final form. AI disrupts this paradigm by necessitating a shift toward a more collaborative and distributed model of authorship, one where the architect acts as a curator, an interpreter, and a systems designer. In this emergent model, design authority arises not from a singular, heroic gesture, but from the intelligent synergy between human intent and machine intelligence. The architect's primary creative act becomes the design of the process itself: curating the data, structuring the workflow, posing the critical questions, and steering the probabilistic outcomes of the AI. This evolution, while technologically novel, finds a fascinating historical precedent in the communal and often anonymous modes of authorship that characterized much of pre-modern building. The construction of Gothic cathedrals by guilds of craftsmen, or the development of vernacular settlements over generations, relied on a shared set of rules and collective intelligence rather than individual genius. In a sense, AI provides a contemporary technological framework for a return to these more collective, process-driven, and inclusive models of creation, de-centering the ego of the lone creator in favor of a rich, hybrid intelligence.

## The Architect's New Roles: Curator, Director, and System Builder

In this evolved paradigm of AI-integrated design, the singular role of the architect metamorphoses into a tripartite operational framework, demanding a fluid mastery of three distinct yet interconnected functions: Curator, Director, and System Builder. As a Curator, the architect exercises critical discernment, navigating the vast, often overwhelming solution space generated by the AI. This is not a passive selection of the most visually appealing option, but an act of deep architectural judgment, identifying and elevating the latent spatial intelligence, programmatic novelty, or contextual resonance from a sea of visual noise. As a Director, the architect engages in an iterative dialogue with the machine, moving from critic to active collaborator. They steer the generative process toward a specific design vision by meticulously refining inputs, adjusting parameters, and providing constant feedback, much like a film director guiding an actor's performance to achieve a desired emotional and narrative effect. Finally, in the most advanced capacity, the architect becomes a System Builder. Here, they transcend the use of existing tools to construct bespoke generative engines, crafting custom algorithmic workflows and, most importantly, curating the foundational datasets that form the AI's "worldview."

## Epistemological Integration: Towards Co-Creative Practice

The most transformative potential of AI in architecture lies beyond the mere layering of machine output and human refinement. It lies in achieving a state of true epistemological integration, an advanced and symbiotic mode of human-machine collaboration. In this state, the distinct ways of "knowing" inherent to both human and machine cease to be sequential inputs and instead become fused into a single, co-creative cognitive system. The machine's capacity for rapid, data-driven permutation and its ability to perceive patterns beyond human intuition are used not just to generate options, but to actively challenge and expand the architect's own creative boundaries. This process thrives on a constant dialectical tension: the architect's reflective judgment, ethical grounding, and search for meaning provides the essential friction against the AI's purely statistical logic, while the AI's unforeseen outputs disrupt the architect's cognitive biases and learned habits. Through this dynamic and continuous interplay, human and artificial intelligences co-evolve. The result is a new, hybrid epistemology, a powerful synthesis where the relentless explorative power of the machine is inextricably woven with the deep, value-driven, and critical capacities of the human mind, simultaneously elevating the potential for radical creative innovation and the profound search for architectural meaning.

## From Theory to Practical Control: A Manifesto for AI-Augmented Architects

The theoretical insights presented in the preceding chapters are not academic endpoints; they are the essential compass required to navigate the technical terrain ahead. Without a critical foundation, the practice of AI in architecture risks becoming a hollow exercise in digital mimicry, a surrender to the algorithmic path of least resistance. Conversely, without practical application, theory remains an impotent abstraction. This section bridges that divide. The following chapters are designed to equip you with the essential techniques to actively, intentionally, and ethically control AI-driven generative processes. To guide this journey from understanding to execution, I propose a set of core tenets for the critically engaged, AI-augmented architect:

1. **Master the Medium.** True creative command begins with a deep, structural understanding of the tools at hand. We must resist the siren call of opaque "black box" interfaces and commit to developing a genuine literacy in the mechanisms of generative AI, its statistical foundations, its operational parameters, and its inherent limitations. Like a traditional artisan who understands the grain of wood or the

cleavage of stone, the AI-augmented architect must learn to navigate the latent space and orchestrate the probabilistic nature of their new medium, transforming it from a magical oracle into a tractable, intelligible material.

2. **Authorship is Redefined, Not Surrendered.** Creative agency in the age of AI is an act of intentionality. We must transition from being passive consumers of algorithmic outputs to becoming active directors of generative systems. Authorship is asserted not in the singular, autographic line, but in the strategic guidance of the entire process, through the careful crafting of prompts, the iterative refinement of control images, and the design of sophisticated feedback loops. Our role is to embed our intent so deeply into the workflow that the AI becomes an extension of our design will, not a substitute for it.
3. **Data Curation is a Foundational Design Act.** We must recognize that the most fundamental design decision occurs before a single image is generated: the curation of data. Datasets are not neutral resources; they are concentrated ideologies. To use them uncritically is to perpetuate the biases, exclusions, and cultural hegemonies they contain. Therefore, the active and critical selection of diverse, inclusive, and context-aware data is an architect's primary ethical and political responsibility. It is an act of epistemological activism that defines the imaginative boundaries of the machine and encodes our values into its very core.
4. **Elevate Architectural Thought.** We must leverage AI as a cognitive liberator, strategically delegating rote, repetitive, and time-consuming tasks to the machine. By automating the generation of schematic variations, rendering studies, or data analysis, we reallocate our most valuable resource—our intellectual and emotional energy—to the domains where human cognition is irreplaceable. This means more time devoted to strategic thinking, empathetic community engagement, complex ethical deliberation, and the profound, human-centered questions of placemaking that define great architecture.
5. **Retain Unwavering Critical Agency.** Finally, the architect must remain the ultimate arbiter of value and meaning. We must cultivate a vigilant, critical skepticism toward all AI-generated outputs, resisting the seduction of the visually plausible but spatially or functionally nonsensical—the occularcentric (El Moussaoui, 2025a). Our most crucial role is to continuously ask the questions the machine cannot: Is this equitable? Is this meaningful? Does this truly serve human life and dignity? This unwavering critical judgment is the final safeguard that preserves the depth, purpose, and soul of our discipline.

With these principles firmly established as our guide, we now move forward from the "why" to the "how"- to the practical, hands-on methodologies to effectively command the immense generative power of artificial intelligence.

# Part 2

## Controlling the Hallucinations— A Practical Guide

# Chapter 9

# Prompt Engineering for Architects

Prompt engineering is the structured practice of crafting precise input queries to guide AI models in generating specific, high-quality outputs. For architects, mastering this skill is essential as it allows them to use AI tools like MidJourney to refine conceptualization, visualization, and representation processes. Unlike traditional software where outputs are dictated by fixed commands, AI-driven design tools rely on linguistic input (text-to-image), making precision in prompts a critical factor in achieving meaningful architectural results. A well-engineered prompt can translate abstract ideas into detailed visualizations, accelerating the design process, expanding creative exploration, and bridging gaps between intention and representation. MidJourney serves as a valuable learning platform due to its balance between user control and AI-driven interpretation, offering a clear demonstration of how textual input directly influences visual form. For this reason, prompt engineering and its application in MidJourney will be the focus of demonstration, illustrating how architects can refine their descriptive precision and develop a disciplined approach to AI-aided design thinking.

## Midjourney

MidJourney is a recent technology, AI-powered text-to-image/text-to-video platform, designed to transform textual prompts into highly realistic and artistic visual outputs. It was developed by a team led by David Holz, who co-founded Leap Motion before establishing MidJourney. The platform debuted in February 2022 and quickly gained traction among creatives, including architects, designers, and visual artists, due to its intuitive usability and capacity to generate high-quality, conceptually rich images.

DOI: 10.1201/9781003637691-11

MidJourney has undergone several iterations, each improving on its predecessor in terms of functionality and output quality:

1. **Version 1 (Feb 2022):** The inaugural release introduced foundational text-to-image capabilities. Outputs were impressionistic, offering atmospheric potential but lacking precision in architectural detail.
2. **Version 2 (April 12, 2022):** This update improved realism and stylistic control, offering a more reliable basis for conceptual visualizations.
3. **Version 3 (July 25, 2022):** Focused on image clarity and finer detailing, this version marked the beginning of MidJourney's usability for schematic architectural ideation.
4. **Version 4 (November 5, 2022):** A transformative upgrade that introduced advanced texture fidelity, accurate spatial perspective, and sharper rendering—making it viable for client-facing imagery.
5. **Version 5 (March 15, 2023):** Delivered major interface improvements, multi-prompt parsing, and heightened contextual specificity.
6. **Version 5.1 (May 3, 2023):** Refined image consistency, style cohesion, and interpretation of compositional complexity.
7. **Version 5.2 (June 22, 2023):** Introduced a new aesthetic ranking system, improved lighting dynamics, and implemented zoom-out functionality for extended spatial compositions.
8. **Version 6 (December 20, 2023):** Marked a qualitative shift in prompt fidelity and photorealism. This release enabled higher coherence in long prompts, empowered detailed remixing of existing images, and enhanced output depth.
9. **Version 6.1 (July 30, 2024):** Optimized scene complexity and personalization. Notably, it introduced user-trained aesthetic preferences, sharper upscalers, and enhanced anatomical rendering (e.g., hands, limbs), reducing common distortions. This version also featured a 25% increase in generation speed and greater textual precision.
10. **Version 7 (April 4, 2025):** This represents a complete architectural overhaul of the platform's generative engine. Version 7 enhanced texture realism, refined image coherence, and introduced a new Draft Mode for accelerated output generation (up to 10× faster at half GPU cost). Crucially, it preserved style-reference codes (srefs) from Version 6.1, ensuring continuity of personalized outputs. Though more capable, it demands refined prompting strategies due to its evolving interpretive behavior.

## From Image to Motion: MidJourney's Video Model (V1)

In June 2025, MidJourney expanded beyond still imagery with the introduction of its first video model, marking a major paradigmatic shift in AI-mediated representation. This new tool allows users to animate images into short, coherent motion sequences, effectively transitioning from static composition to temporal visual narration.

- The feature, accessible via the web interface (not Discord), enables a single image—generated via prompt or uploaded manually—to be extended into a 5-second video.
- Users may continue the animation for up to 21 seconds in 4-second increments, choosing between *low motion* (subtle ambient shifts) or *high motion* (integrated camera and object movement).
- A generative interpolation system creates smooth transitions between frames, maintaining stylistic integrity and spatial consistency.
- While early, this development opens new terrain for architectural experimentation—allowing not just for the visualization of designed forms, but the simulation of atmospheres, temporal transitions, and experiential narratives.

The video model is currently computationally intensive, using approximately eight times the GPU minutes of static images. It is available to paid users, with upscaling and further refinement tools under progressive release.

## Underlying Model Architecture: From GANs to Diffusion

While MidJourney originally resembled Generative Adversarial Network (GAN) frameworks, its later iterations—especially from Version 5 onward—have increasingly adopted diffusion-based architectures, in alignment with broader trends in image synthesis technologies. These models operate through iterative denoising of latent spaces, guided by transformer-based language encoders, such as those found in OpenAI's GPT family. The system can be broadly understood as a two-phase pipeline:

1. **Text Encoding:** Prompts are interpreted by a natural language processing model that parses semantic meaning, stylistic cues, and compositional intent.

2. **Image/Video Generation:** Encoded data is then passed into a denoising diffusion model, which reconstructs visual outputs through probabilistic refinement. This architecture enables greater nuance, resolution, and fidelity than earlier GAN-based techniques.

The dataset upon which MidJourney is trained remains proprietary but is believed to draw on vast quantities of publicly available image corpora, artistic sources, and architectural photographs. The developers claim compliance with copyright laws and ethical data acquisition protocols.

# Chapter 10

# MidJourney Interfaces
## Discord vs. Web Platform

MidJourney operates across two principal environments: the Discord command interface and the midjourney.com web platform (Table 3). While both provide access to the same generative models and core functionality, they differ substantially in terms of operational structure, user interaction modes, and practical affordances for iterative image production.

## Discord Interface

The Discord implementation is command-line oriented. Prompts are issued via slash commands (e.g., /imagine), with parameters appended manually using text-based syntax. Users engage with the system in a semi-programmatic manner, writing structured commands to control resolution, style, aspect ratio, model version, and other image attributes (Fig. 3).

This interface offers access to the full suite of MidJourney's advanced functionalities. Notably:

- Users can deploy commands such as /blend, /describe, /shorten, and /tune, which are not yet available through the web interface.
- Prompt structure is fully transparent, requiring precise user input for all parameters. This is particularly valuable in educational contexts, where it encourages clarity and control over generative behavior.
- Style Tuners and Option Sets can only be created and managed via Discord.
- Discord also permits full deletion of generated images, a critical feature for managing intellectual property or sensitive content.

DOI: 10.1201/9781003637691-12

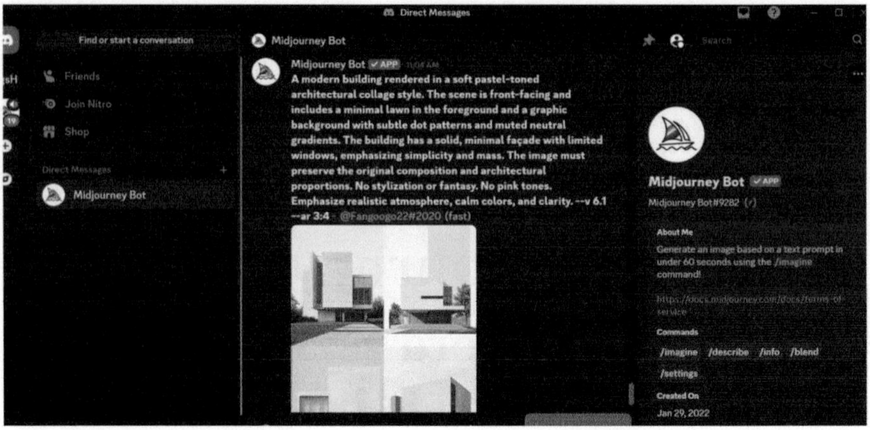


**Figure 3.** Midjourney discord interface.

- Community features such as shared prompting channels allow users to view and analyze others' prompts and outputs in real time, fostering prompt literacy and technique sharing.

However, image manipulation operations such as cropping, panning, zooming, or region-based inpainting require separate steps or post-processing via external tools or commands.

## Web Interface (midjourney.com)

The web platform provides a consolidated graphical interface. Prompts are entered into a dedicated UI, and parameter adjustments are performed via toggles, dropdowns, or sliders rather than typed syntax. Images are displayed within a personal gallery, with generation history and prompt metadata accessible for each image (Fig. 4).

Distinct functionalities include:

- The Editor, which integrates tools for cropping, panning, inpainting (Vary Region), and aspect ratio adjustment into a single workspace. This enables more granular and immediate post-processing of generated outputs.
- Image references can be uploaded directly and assigned roles such as prompt image, style reference, or omni reference via visual selection tools.
- Personalized profiles—trained on prior output preferences—can be selected and managed visually. These profiles persist across sessions and streamline aesthetic continuity.

**Figure 4.** Midjourney web-interface.

- Prompt reuse tools are built into the interface, allowing users to re-issue a prior prompt, remix an image, or apply an existing style with a single click.
- Users can toggle publication status (Publish/Unpublish) for each image post-generation.

Unlike Discord, the web interface does not allow image deletion, nor does it offer access to certain experimental commands such as /blend, /shorten, or /tune.

## Comparative Summary

**Table 3.** Comparative summary of midjourney's different interface usage.

| Feature | Discord Bot | Web Interface |
|---|---|---|
| Prompt Input | Command-based (/imagine, etc.) | UI-based text entry |
| Parameter Specification | Manual syntax input (--ar, etc.) | Button and slider-based |
| Reference Image Upload | Requires hosted URL | Direct upload and assignment |
| Inpainting and Editing | Limited to separate steps | Fully integrated editor |
| Style Tuners/Option Sets | Created and edited | Can be used but not created |
| Personalized Profile Management | Requires commands | Managed visually |
| Image Deletion | Fully supported | Not available |
| Image Publication Control | Not available | Toggle publish/unpublish |
| Prompt Reuse | Manual copy or remix | Integrated reuse tools |
| Speed Modes | Full access | Full access |
| Video Generation | Web-only (as of V1, June 2025) | Web-only |

## Recommendations

The Discord interface is better suited for users requiring fine-grained control over prompt syntax, batch experimentation, or access to advanced and experimental features. It is particularly valuable in academic settings where the pedagogical emphasis lies on understanding the logic of prompting and prompt structuring.

The web interface, by contrast, is optimized for visual workflows. It supports rapid iteration, integrated post-processing, and smoother user experience. It is especially useful for applied design tasks, presentation preparation, and generating cohesive visual series within a controlled interface.

Both environments complement one another and can be used in parallel depending on project phase and user needs.

Chapter 11

# MidJourney Discord Commands

## Annotated Overview

MidJourney's Discord implementation includes a set of structured slash commands that allow users to generate images, manage settings, create stylistic tuners, and engage with their generation history. These commands are foundational for prompt-based workflows, particularly when aiming to maintain control over parameters, reference behavior, and stylistic output.

**/imagine**

**Function:** Primary image generation command. Accepts a textual prompt with optional parameters.

**Application:** Core to all workflows; serves as the entry point for concept generation, atmospheric studies, and iterative visualization.

**Syntax:**

/imagine prompt: "Futuristic library with cantilevered terraces at sunset --ar 16:9 --v 6"

**/blend**

**Function:** Combines two or more images into a hybrid composition.

**Application:** Useful for merging spatial typologies, materials, or atmospheres across projects. A powerful tool in speculative form-making and design precedent studies.

**Note:** Only available in Discord; images must be uploaded directly.

DOI: 10.1201/9781003637691-13

**/describe**

**Function:** Upload an image and receive four prompt suggestions that likely produced it.

**Application:** Supports reverse engineering of outputs, stylistic studies, and teaching prompt deconstruction. Especially useful in unpacking aesthetic tendencies or material language from reference images.

**/tune**

**Function:** Generates a "Style Tuner" based on a provided prompt. The user selects preferred variations, and a new stylistic profile is saved.

**Application:** Enables development of **customized visual signatures** over time—relevant in maintaining brand coherence or thematic consistency across competitions, portfolios, or projects.

**/list_tuners**

**Function:** Lists all saved Style Tuners associated with the user account.

**Application:** Helps maintain a working archive of aesthetic grammars. Useful in managing parallel projects or collaborative work with predefined styles.

**/prefer remix**

**Function:** Enables or disables Remix Mode. When active, the "Vary (Strong)" button on outputs allows live editing of prompt content and parameters.

**Application:** Encourages exploratory prompting and midstream redirection of architectural ideas without restarting the entire workflow.

**/prefer suffix**

**Function:** Appends a designated suffix to every prompt.

**Application:** Automates the consistent application of model version, style, or resolution preferences across prompts. Useful for batch production.

**Example:**

/prefer suffix: --ar 16:9 --v 6

**/shorten**

**Function:** Analyzes a long prompt and suggests simplified alternatives.

**Application:** Trains concise descriptive expression—valuable in early-phase concept articulation or when testing prompt minimalism.

**/synonyms**

**Function:** Offers alternative terms or variations for a given keyword in the prompt.

**Application:** Facilitates lexical diversity in design expression, enhancing stylistic flexibility or resolving prompt stagnation.

**/settings**

**Function:** Opens a visual panel to toggle default parameters such as model version, Remix Mode, Public/Stealth settings, and quality presets.

**Application:** Provides a quick interface for reconfiguring working conditions without command syntax.

**/fast, /relax, /turbo**

**Function:** Switches between GPU speed modes.

- /fast: Regular GPU processing (default for most users)
- /relax: Slower rendering, but no GPU cost (Pro/Mega only)
- /turbo: Fastest rendering, reduced fine detail

**Application:** Helps balance image generation priorities across time-sensitive tasks, large batch rendering, or exploratory sketching.

**/show**

**Function:** Regenerates an image from its Job ID.

**Application:** Useful for revisiting specific outputs, documenting variations, or archiving outputs with accurate parameter tracing.

**/info**

**Function:** Displays user information including job queue, remaining GPU time, plan details, and current mode.

**Application:** Useful in teaching resource management and understanding computational cost structures of generative workflows.

**/subscribe, /public, /stealth, /invite**

**Function:** Account and visibility management.

- /subscribe: Opens user's subscription page
- /public / /stealth: Controls image visibility
- /invite: Generates Discord server invite link

**Application:** Mostly administrative, but relevant for managing project confidentiality and workflow environments.

Chapter 12

# Architectural Scenarios and Command Applications in Discord

MidJourney's command system is not just an interface for image generation—it can be actively integrated into the architectural workflow, from early speculative ideation to stylistic calibration and formal iteration. Below are illustrative scenarios that demonstrate how architects might apply specific commands or parameters to navigate design tasks using the Discord interface.

## Conceptual Diversification: /imagine + --repeat + --chaos

**Scenario:** A studio exploring alternatives for a civic building typology (e.g., library, town hall, museum) wants to rapidly visualize conceptual variations.

**Workflow:**

/imagine prompt: "A civic library surrounded by water, Brutalist style --ar 16:9 --chaos 60 --repeat 4" (Fig. 5).

**Purpose:** Using --repeat with --chaos allows students or designers to produce eight distinct interpretations of the same brief. This becomes a generative matrix from which promising formal directions may be selected.

DOI: 10.1201/9781003637691-14

**Figure 5.** Midjourney discord interface using "A civic library surrounded by water, Brutalist style --ar 16:9 --chaos 60 --repeat 4" prompt.

## Precedent Blending: /blend

**Scenario:** The architect wants to fuse two spatial archetypes—say, a traditional riad courtyard and a modernist villa—into a single image that expresses both spatial languages.

**Workflow:**

/blend [image of architecture 1] [image of a architecture 2] (Fig. 6).

**Purpose:** Enables hybrid thinking without needing to articulate the fusion in language. Offers visual speculation before programmatic commitment.

**Figure 6.** Using the blend command between image 1 (top right) and image 2 (top left).

## Prompt Tuning for Style Fidelity: /tune + /prefer suffix

**Scenario:** A researcher develops a recognizable style across a series of competition boards and wants consistency in materiality, composition, and atmosphere.

**Workflow:**

/tune prompt: "A low-carbon timber pavilion in a foggy forest"

→ Select preferred variations

→ Save as Style Tuner: "foggy-timber"

/prefer suffix: --sref foggy-timber --ar 2:3 --v 6 (Fig. 7)

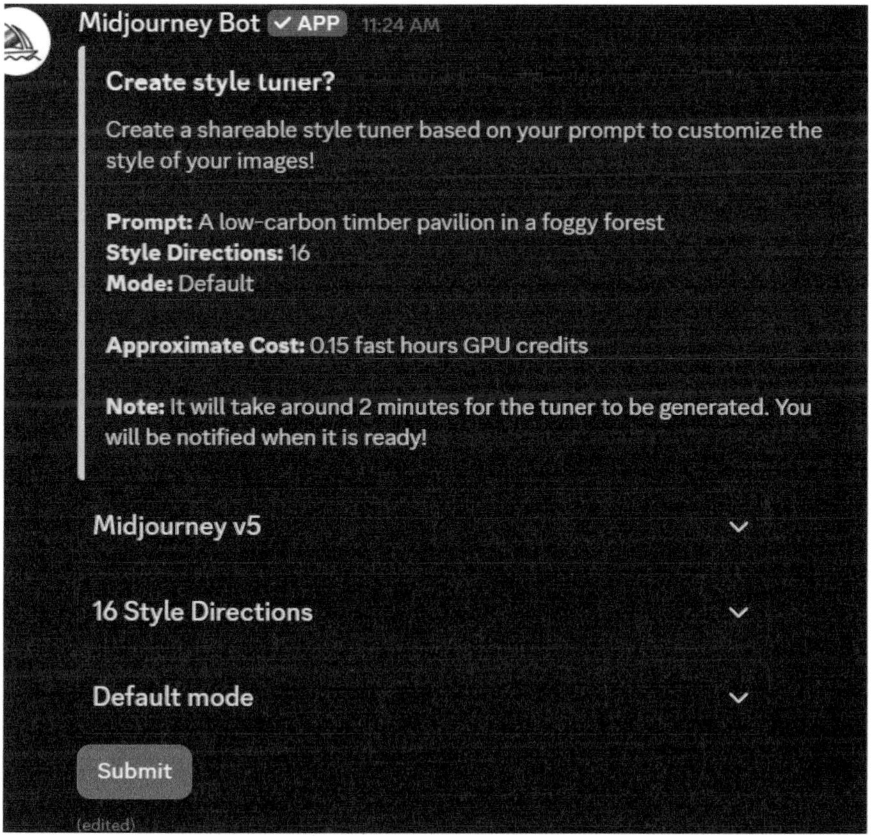


**Figure 7.** Creating a style reference.

**Purpose:** Ensures that every future prompt is automatically filtered through the same stylistic lens. Useful in multi-phase projects or portfolio development.

## Reverse Prompt Engineering: /describe

**Scenario:** A student finds a compelling image of a megastructure and wishes to understand how it might be reconstructed through prompt logic.

**Workflow:**

/describe [upload image]

**Purpose:** Generates four different prompts based on the uploaded image. These serve as heuristic tools to understand how MidJourney interprets

**Figure 8.** Using the describe command of the image above. The text provided under are the 4 different description midjourney have provided.

composition, material, scale, and atmosphere. It also trains prompt fluency by revealing hidden syntactic structures (Fig. 8).

1. *A modern and minimalistic Arabian-inspired architecture with tall white columns and arches, a large window at the end of an open doorway leading to the outside, a glossy marble floor, and a symmetrical composition. The image appears to be a hyper-realistic photograph.*
2. *An empty hall with white marble columns and arched windows, a modern minimalist architectural style, with the view of the Alhambra Palace in a Ramadan-themed photorealistic rendering, in daylight, high resolution, hyper-realistic, and cinematic.*
3. *Interior view of the entrance to an Arabian palace, with white marble columns featuring dark beige patterns. The architecture is modern and symmetrical, with a large arched window in the background. The scene is photorealistic in style.*
4. *3D rendering of modern Islamic architecture, a symmetrical composition with a marble floor featuring a subtle texture. Tall arched doorways lead to an open space outside, with light and shadow creating depth in the scene. The architectural design style includes detailed ornamentation on columns and arches, resulting in a minimalist yet elegant atmosphere. The focus is on geometric shapes and straight lines for symmetry, with high-resolution and realistic details.*

## Curated Variations Through Interactive Editing: /prefer remix

**Scenario:** A faculty member is guiding students through variations of a proposed architectural design. Rather than rewriting prompts, they want students to focus on subtle shifts (materials, lighting, density).

**Workflow:**

Enable:

/prefer remix (Fig. 9).

Then use the "Vary (Strong)" button on an image and modify the text:

"Public square with travertine paving and pergola structures, evening light"
→ Remix:

"Public square with basalt paving and tensile canopies, rainy atmosphere"

**Purpose:** Facilitates iterative formal studies while anchoring the original compositional framework.

**Figure 9.** Zone editing.

## Sketch Output with Partial Rendering: --stop

**Scenario:** During schematic design discussions, the team wants representations that suggest atmosphere and form without full resolution—mimicking the ambiguity of hand sketches.

**Workflow:**

/imagine prompt: "Linear housing scheme in a dry riverbed --stop 55" (Fig. 10).

**NOTE:** that –stop is still not compatible with version 7.0 so version 6/5/4/3/2 must be added to the text

**Purpose:** Output appears as a "half-rendered" image—suggestive and open-ended. Useful for stakeholder engagement in early design discussions where over-definition might constrain conversation.

**Figure 10.** Partial renders by playing with the percentage of steps.

## Prompt Economy and Optimization: /shorten + /synonyms

**Scenario:** In a prompt-heavy design sprint, efficiency becomes essential. The designer wants to compress verbose descriptions while testing semantic substitutions for refinement.

**Workflow:**

/shorten prompt: "A hyperdense vertical city formed of crystalline tubes with interlaced walkways and vertical agriculture systems" (Fig. 11).

/synonyms: "crystalline"

**Purpose:** Helps identify core linguistic drivers of generative output. Encourages lexical experimentation and clarity of intent.

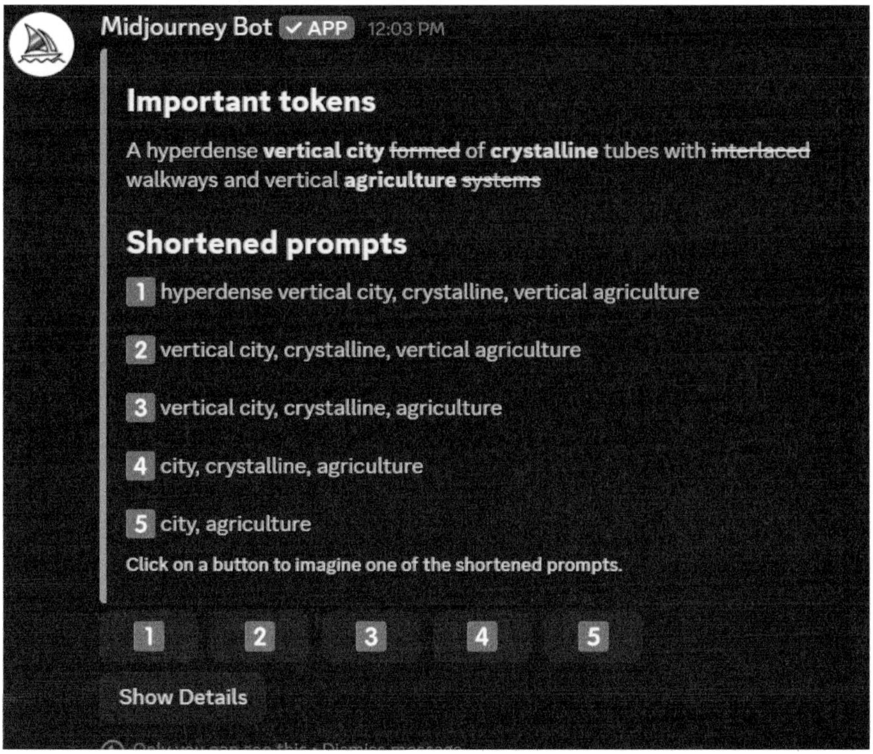


**Figure 11.** Prompt shortening command.

Chapter 13

# Prompt Engineering Components

## Core Components of a MidJourney Prompt

1. **Primary Description**: The core subject or scene you want the AI to generate. This should be clear and provide enough context for the AI to understand the main focus.
   - **Example**: "A futuristic villa" (Fig. 12)
2. **Detail and Attributes**: Specific features, materials, or elements that you want included in the image. This can help the AI refine the output.

**Example**: "A futuristic villa with sleek, flowing organic shapes, large glass walls, rooftop gardens, and glowing ambient lights. The villa features a cantilevered design overlooking a serene water body, with integrated solar panels and lush greenery surrounding the structure --ar 16:9 --v 6 --q 5 --s 800" (Fig. 13)

3. **Style and Mood Modifiers**: These modifiers define the artistic style, mood, or atmosphere you want in the image.
   - **Example**: "A futuristic villa with flowing organic shapes, glowing neon accents, and large reflective glass panels. Set in a cyberpunk style, the villa is surrounded by mist and illuminated by vibrant lights, creating a bold, dramatic atmosphere --ar 2:3 --v 5 --s 1000 (Fig. 14)
4. **Contextual Modifiers**: Elements that set the context, like location, lighting, weather, or specific environments.
   - **Example**: "Set on a cliffside overlooking the ocean, the futuristic villa is bathed in soft dusk lighting. The scene features surrounding vegetation and a private infinity pool, emphasizing tranquility and elegance" (Fig. 15)

DOI: 10.1201/9781003637691-15

**Figure 12.** Using the "a futuristic villa"prompt.

**Figure 13.** Using "A futuristic villa with sleek, flowing organic shapes, large glass walls, rooftop gardens, and glowing ambient lights. The villa features a cantilevered design overlooking a serene water body, with integrated solar panels and lush greenery surrounding the structure --ar 16:9 --v 6 --q 5 --s 800." Prompt.

**Figure 14.** Using "A futuristic villa with flowing organic shapes, glowing neon accents, and large reflective glass panels. Set in a cyberpunk style, the villa is surrounded by mist and illuminated by vibrant lights, creating a bold, dramatic atmosphere --ar 2:3 --v 5 --s 1000." prompt.

### Structuring an Effective Prompt

When creating prompts for MidJourney, think of the prompt as a set of instructions that gradually refine the AI's focus. The general structure can be broken down into the following components:

1. **Primary Subject (What)**: Clearly state what you want to generate.
   - Example: "A futuristic cityscape"
2. **Attributes (Details about the Subject)**: Add descriptive elements that define the subject's features.
   - Example: "A futuristic cityscape with neon lights, flying cars, and glass skyscrapers"

**Figure 15.** Prompt used "Set on a cliffside overlooking the ocean, the futuristic villa is bathed in soft dusk lighting. The scene features surrounding vegetation and a private infinity pool, emphasizing tranquility and elegance."

3. **Contextual Elements (Where/When)**: Add details about the environment, time of day, or other contextual settings.
   - Example: "A futuristic cityscape with neon lights, flying cars, and glass skyscrapers, at night, in a bustling urban setting"
4. **Stylistic Modifiers (How)**: Specify the artistic style, medium, or mood to influence the overall appearance.
   - Example: "A futuristic cityscape with neon lights, flying cars, and glass skyscrapers, at night, in a bustling urban setting, cyberpunk style"
5. **Special Parameters (Optional)**: Fine-tune the output using parameters.
   - Example: "A futuristic cityscape with neon lights, flying cars, and glass skyscrapers, at night, in a bustling urban setting, cyberpunk style --ar 16:9 --v 5 --q 4 --s 1000"

## Important Tips for Structuring Prompts

1. **Be Specific but Not Overly Restrictive**: While details are helpful, overly complex prompts may confuse the model or produce mixed results. Focus on key elements that matter most.
2. **Iterative Refinement**: Start with a simple prompt and gradually add or adjust details based on the generated output.
3. **Order of Words Matters**: MidJourney often prioritizes the first elements of the prompt, so place the most important information at the beginning.
4. **Use Style and Mood Modifiers Thoughtfully**: Experiment with terms like "photorealistic," "watercolor," "low-poly," "dark fantasy," "surreal," etc., to see how they influence the output.
5. **Experiment with Negative Prompts (using --no)**: Specify what elements you don't want to appear to refine your output further.
    - o Example: "A futuristic cityscape with neon lights --no rain"

**Let us look into more details on how Midjourney's parameters and the difference of output.**

When working with MidJourney, the basic prompt structure starts with a clear description of the desired image. A well-crafted prompt should be as specific as needed to guide the AI while leaving room for creative interpretation when appropriate.

- **Example**: "A futuristic cityscape at sunset, with flying cars and neon lights" (Fig. 16)

Special Prompt Modifiers and Their Impact

Aspect Ratio (--ar)

- **Purpose**: Specifies the aspect ratio of the generated image.
- **Syntax**: --ar [width:height]
- **Examples**:
    - o --ar 16:9: Generates a wide image suitable for cinematic scenes or panoramic landscapes.
    - o --ar 1:1: Creates a square image, ideal for focused compositions or profile shots.
    - o **Effect**: Aspect ratios affect the overall composition and framing of the scene. A wide aspect ratio can emphasize horizontal elements (e.g., landscapes), while a tall aspect ratio might highlight verticality (e.g., towers, tall buildings).

**Figure 16.** Prompt used "A futuristic cityscape at sunset, with flying cars and neon lights".

Model Version (--v)

- **Purpose**: Selects a specific version of the MidJourney model to use. Different versions may produce variations in style, detail, and artistic interpretation.
- **Syntax**: --v [number]
- **Examples**:
  - --v 6: Uses version 6 of the model, which may focus on more realistic outputs and refined details.
  - **Effect**: Choosing a model version can impact the image style, from photorealism to more stylized artistic interpretations. Experimenting with different versions helps find the one that best suits the project's needs (Fig. 17).

Quality (--q)

- **Purpose**: Controls the amount of processing time and effort the AI dedicates to generating the image.
- **Syntax**: --q [number]

**Figure 17.** Using variable versions from version 2 to version 6, left to right.

- **Examples**:
  - --q 2: Standard quality.
  - --q 5: Higher quality, resulting in more detailed and refined images but with longer rendering times.

**Effect**: Increasing quality enhances the richness of details and complexity, while lower settings may produce quicker, less detailed outputs (Fig. 18)

Stylize (--s)

- **Purpose**: Adjusts how strongly artistic elements influence the image generation.
- **Syntax**: --s [number]
- **Examples**:
  - --s 1000: High stylization, which may produce a more painterly or artistic output.
  - --s 0: Minimal stylization, focusing more on realism.

**Figure 18.** Same prompt for both, on the left with -- q2 on the right -- q5.

**Figure 19.** Prompt used for both images: A futuristic building in a high-tech city, with flowing organic shapes, integrated greenery, and glowing lights. Surrounded by advanced infrastructure such as skybridges and platforms for flying vehicle. The image on the left --seed 40 --s 1000 on the right seed 40 --s 0.

 - **Effect**: This parameter controls the artistic "flair" in images, making them more or less abstract or stylized. High values are ideal for creating art-like images, while lower values suit realism-focused projects.

Seed (--seed)

- **Purpose**: Sets a specific random seed to reproduce consistent results across generations.
- **Syntax**: --seed [number]
- **Examples**:
  - --seed 42: Reproduces the same image output when using the same prompt and parameters (Fig. 19)

**Effect**: Controlling the seed ensures consistency across outputs, useful for iterative refinement.

## Advanced Prompt Elements for MidJourney

### Camera Settings and Perspective

- **Purpose**: Simulate specific photographic techniques, lenses, or perspectives to influence the visual style and composition.
- **Syntax Examples**:
  - "Shot with a 35mm lens" or "Wide-angle lens": Influences the field of view, depth of field, and distortion effects.

**Figure 20.** A futuristic building in a high-tech city, with flowing organic shapes, integrated greenery, and glowing lights. Surrounded by advanced infrastructure such as skybridges and platforms for flying vehicle. wide-angle lens/Shot with a 35 mm lens --seed 40 --s 1000 --v 6.1 on the left (wide-angle lens) on the right (Shot with a 35 mm lens) – the rest are the same prompt parameters used.

  - "Aerial view" or "Bird's eye view": Alters the perspective, useful for architectural renders or landscapes.
  - "Macro shot": Focuses on close-up details with high precision.
- **Effect**: Camera modifiers affect how the AI "frames" the scene, creating different levels of depth, focus, and context. A macro shot will emphasize fine textures, while a wide-angle view emphasizes context and spatial relationships (Fig. 20)

**Lighting Modifiers**

- **Purpose**: Control the lighting conditions in the generated image.
- **Syntax Examples**:
  - "Golden hour lighting": Produces warm, soft light typical of sunrise or sunset.
  - "Neon lights" or "Moody lighting": Specifies artificial or atmospheric light sources (Fig. 21)
- **Effect**: Lighting greatly affects mood, realism, and focus. Soft lighting adds warmth, while dramatic lighting can introduce strong contrast and tension.

**Artistic and Style Modifiers**

- **Purpose**: Shape the artistic style or medium used in the image generation.

**Figure 21.** A futuristic building in a high-tech city, with flowing organic shapes, integrated greenery, and glowing lights. Surrounded by advanced infrastructure such as skybridges and platforms for flying vehicle. wide-angle lens/Shot with a 35 mm lens --seed 40 on the left (Green Neon Lights) on the right (Golden hour lighting) – the rest are the same prompt parameters used.

- **Syntax Examples**:
  - "In the style of Impressionist painting"
  - "Concept art style"
  - "Photorealistic render"
- **Effect**: Style modifiers direct the AI to emulate specific artistic movements, aesthetics, or realism levels, allowing precise control over visual presentation (Fig. 22)

Figure 22 An impressionist painting of a futuristic building in a high-tech city, featuring flowing organic shapes and integrated greenery. The scene is painted with soft brush strokes, vivid and fragmented colors, and a dreamlike quality typical of impressionist. Advanced infrastructure surrounds the building, including skybridges and platforms for flying vehicles, blending into the artistic style. --s 750 --v 5.2

Color Palettes and Textures

- **Purpose**: Influence colors, textures, and overall visual cohesion.
- **Syntax Examples**:
  - "Muted earth tones with rough textures"
  - "Vibrant colors with smooth metallic surfaces"
- **Effect**: Color and texture modifiers control visual harmony, helping achieve specific moods or atmospheres in the output (Fig. 23)

**Figure 22.** An impressionist painting of a futuristic building in a high-tech city, featuring flowing organic shapes and integrated greenery. The scene is painted with soft brush strokes, vivid and fragmented colors, and a dreamlike quality typical of impressionist. Advanced infrastructure surrounds the building, including skybridges and platforms for flying vehicles, blending into the artistic style. --s 750 --v 5.2.

## Prompt Variations for Different Results: How to Fine-Tune Your Outputs

Prompt variations are a powerful way to influence the outputs generated by text-to-image AI models. By adjusting your prompts with different descriptors, styles, or modifiers, you can guide the AI to produce outputs that align closely with your intentions.

1. **Varying Descriptive Details**

- **Base Prompt**: "A modern house with large windows" (Fig. 24)
- **Variation 1 (Adding Material)**: "A modern house with large windows, made of concrete and wood"

**Figure 23.** A futuristic building in a high-tech city, featuring flowing organic shapes with smooth metallic surfaces that reflect vibrant colors. The scene is rendered in the style of an impressionist painting, with soft brush strokes, a dreamlike quality, and an artistic play of light and shadow. Advanced infrastructure, including skybridges and platforms for flying vehicles, blends harmoniously into the composition. --seed 40 --s 1000 --v 6.0.

**Figure 24.** "A modern house with large windows, made of concrete and wood". On the left "A modern house with large windows, surrounded by a dense forest" on the right.

   - **Effect**: This prompt specifies the materials, influencing the AI to add concrete and wood textures to the structure.
- **Variation 2 (Adding Environment)**: "A modern house with large windows, surrounded by a dense forest"
   - **Effect**: By adding the environment descriptor, the AI situates the house within a forest setting, changing the context and potentially adding natural lighting or shadows.

2. **Changing the Style or Theme**

- **Base Prompt**: "A futuristic cityscape" (Fig. 25)
- **Variation 1 (Cyberpunk Style)**: "A futuristic cityscape with neon lights, flying cars, and a dark, rainy atmosphere in cyberpunk style"
   - **Effect**: The prompt directs the AI to generate a cyberpunk-themed cityscape with vibrant neon colors and a moody, rain-soaked atmosphere.
- **Variation 2 (Minimalist Style)**: ""
   - **Effect**: This variation guides the AI toward simplicity, emphasizing minimalism with clean design, open spaces, and limited color use.

3. **Adjusting Perspective and Camera Angles**

- **Base Prompt**: "A grand staircase inside a palace" (Fig. 26)
- **Variation 1 (Aerial View)**: "A grand staircase inside a palace, viewed from bird's eye view"
   - **Effect**: This variation changes the perspective, guiding the AI to show the staircase from a bird's eye view, which can highlight symmetry or architectural layout.

**Figure 25.** On the right "A futuristic cityscape with neon lights, flying cars, and a dark, rainy atmosphere in cyberpunk style". On the left Minimilistic Style.

- **Variation 2 (Close-Up View)**: "A grand staircase inside a palace, close-up view of the intricate railing details"
  - **Effect**: Here, the focus is on close details, such as the railing, creating a more intimate and detailed image.

4. **Modifying Lighting Conditions**

- **Base Prompt**: "An ancient temple in the jungle" (Fig. 27)
- **Variation 1 (Nighttime Lighting)**: "An ancient temple in the jungle, illuminated by the moonlight"
  - **Effect**: This lighting change shifts the atmosphere to a nocturnal setting, with the AI adding cool tones, shadows, and moonlit highlights.

**Figure 26.** On the left "A grand staircase inside a palace, viewed from bird's eye view". On the right: "A grand staircase inside a palace, close-up view of the intricate railing details".

**Figure 27.** On the left "An ancient temple in the jungle, illuminated by the moonlight". On the right: "An ancient temple in the jungle, illuminated with a soft light of sunset or sunrise".

- **Variation 2 (Golden Hour)**: ""
    - o **Effect**: The prompt creates a warm, soft lighting effect typical of sunrise or sunset, giving the image a serene and glowing ambiance.

## Focusing on Artistic Styles

- **Base Prompt**: "A portrait of a warrior" (Fig. 28)
- **Variation 1 (Renaissance Style)**: "A portrait of a warrior in Renaissance painting style"
    - o **Effect**: This prompt directs the AI to mimic the style of a Renaissance painting, adding historical details like clothing, textures, and colors typical of the period.
- **Variation 2 (Comic Book Style)**: "A portrait of a warrior in comic book style with bold lines and vibrant colors"
    - o **Effect**: This variation results in a dynamic, graphic representation with exaggerated features, bold lines, and vibrant color contrasts.

**Figure 28.** On the left: "A portrait of a warrior in Renaissance painting style". On the right: "A portrait of a warrior in comic book style with bold lines and vibrant colors".

## Adjusting Aspect Ratios for Composition

- **Base Prompt**: "A tranquil beach scene" (Fig. 29)
- **Variation 1 (Wide Aspect Ratio)**: "A tranquil beach scene --ar 16:9"
    - o **Effect**: The wide aspect ratio emphasizes the horizontal elements, capturing more of the beach, horizon, and sky.
- **Variation 2 (Tall Aspect Ratio)**: "A tranquil beach scene --ar 9:16"
    - o **Effect**: This tall aspect ratio focuses on vertical elements, potentially highlighting palm trees, cliffs, or tall waves.

## Using Mood and Emotion Modifiers

- **Base Prompt**: "A medieval castle on a hill" (Fig. 30)
- **Variation 1 (Mysterious Atmosphere)**: "A medieval castle on a hill, surrounded by dense fog and eerie lighting"
    - **Effect**: The AI produces an image with a mysterious, moody atmosphere, using fog and low light to create tension.
- **Variation 2 (Peaceful Setting)**: "A medieval castle on a hill, with clear skies and birds flying around"
    - **Effect**: This variation introduces a serene and peaceful vibe, using clear skies and wildlife to alter the emotional tone.

**Figure 29.** Up: "A tranquil beach scene --ar 16:9". On the right "A tranquil beach scene --ar 9:16".

## Emphasizing Textures and Materials

- **Base Prompt**: "A traditional Japanese house" (Fig. 31)
- **Variation 1 (Wood and Paper)**: "A traditional Japanese house with wooden beams and paper sliding doors"
    - **Effect**: The AI emphasizes wood textures and traditional paper elements, giving the structure authenticity.

**Figure 30.** On the left "A medieval castle on a hill, surrounded by dense fog and eerie lighting". On the right: "A medieval castle on a hill, with clear skies and birds flying around".

**Figure 31.** On the left: "A traditional Japanese house with wooden beams and paper sliding doors". On the right: "A traditional Japanese house made with glass and steel elements".

- **Variation 2 (Modern Materials)**: "A traditional Japanese house made with glass and steel elements"
  - **Effect**: This prompt creates a fusion of traditional design with modern materials, producing a unique architectural interpretation.

## Negative Prompts for Refinement

- **Base Prompt**: "A bustling market in a Middle Eastern city" (Fig. 32)
- **Negative Prompt Variation**: "A bustling market in a Middle Eastern city --no modern clothing, no vehicles"

**Figure 32.** On the left: "A bustling market in a Middle Eastern city". On the right: "A bustling market in a Middle Eastern city --no modern clothing, no vehicles".

- o **Effect**: This variation ensures the scene remains historically or culturally authentic by excluding modern elements.

## Experimenting with Specific Genres or Themes

- **Base Prompt**: "A fantasy castle" (Fig. 33)
- **Variation 1 (Steampunk Theme)**: "A fantasy castle with steampunk gears, pipes, and steam, under a cloudy sky"
    - o **Effect**: The AI blends the fantasy castle design with steampunk aesthetics, adding gears, pipes, and other thematic elements.

**Figure 33.** On the left: "A fantasy castle with steampunk gears, pipes, and steam, under a cloudy sky". On the right: "A fantasy castle made of ice and snow, glowing under northern lights".

- **Variation 2 (Ice Theme)**: "A fantasy castle made of ice and snow, glowing under northern lights"
  - **Effect**: This prompt creates an ethereal ice castle with a glowing ambiance, leveraging the northern lights for dramatic lighting.

## Different Parameters

### *--chaos: Controlling Variation and Surprise*

The --chaos parameter adjusts the degree of randomness in MidJourney's image generation process. By default, the system attempts to produce the most probable or coherent interpretation of a prompt. With --chaos, however, you can dial up the unpredictability of the output.

- **Range:** --chaos 0 (least variation) to --chaos 100 (maximum variation)
- **Short form:** --c

#### What It Does

Lower values keep the results more stable and focused, useful for refining a known concept. Higher values introduce diverse, unexpected interpretations, ideal for concept generation, speculative thinking, or creative experimentation.

#### Example

"A high-tech monastery in a desert --ar 16:9 --chaos 15"

Produces similar compositions with minor changes.

"A high-tech monastery in a desert --ar 16:9 --chaos 80"

Produces outputs that may diverge radically in form, color, or spatial arrangement.

#### When to Use It

- Use low chaos for consistency and detail control during design development.
- Use medium to high chaos to stimulate creativity, especially in early stages of architectural ideation where surprise is valuable.

This parameter is especially useful in teaching design students the value of design iteration beyond control—exploring how variation can lead to new architectural ideas that may not have been anticipated.

### *--repeat: Batch Prompt Execution*

The --repeat parameter allows you to run the same prompt multiple times in one command, generating a batch of image sets in parallel.

It is particularly useful for comparative exploration, where designers want to see how the same input may lead to diverse visual outcomes due to stochastic variation in the model.

- **Syntax:** --repeat [number] or --r [number]
- **Range:** Up to 40 (limited by subscription tier)

**Example**

"Futuristic market square at sunset --repeat 5"

This will generate five independent interpretations of the same prompt.

**When to Use It**

Ideal during early design phases when exploring mood, typology, or compositional diversity without rewriting the prompt.

### *--weird: Pushing Aesthetic Boundaries*

The --weird parameter invites MidJourney to push the image generation beyond normative interpretation—yielding strange, alien, or idiosyncratic visuals. It is especially productive for speculative design, critical design research, or worldbuilding exercises.

- **Syntax:** --weird [number] or --w [number]
- **Range:** 0–3000 (recommended 250–2000)

**Example**

"Urban ruin in post-apocalyptic Venice --weird 1500"

**When to Use It**

Useful when conventional architectural representations are insufficient, and the designer seeks subversive form-making or radical aesthetic departures.

### *--stop: Partial Rendering Control*

The --stop parameter interrupts the image generation process at a specified percentage of completion. It is useful for producing sketch-like, gestural visuals or for studying the early evolution of the generated form.

- **Syntax:** --stop [number]
- **Range:** 10–100 (percentage of completion)

**Example**

"Parametric museum in the desert --stop 70"

**When to Use It**

Helpful when aiming for a non-finished, conceptual rendering or for emphasizing abstraction over resolution. Also pedagogically valuable for teaching iterative visual development.

### *--raw: Bypass Aesthetic Filters*

The --raw parameter disables the default aesthetic bias that MidJourney applies to prompt interpretation. It allows for a more literal translation of the text prompt, often yielding outputs that are less "art-directed" and more direct.

- **Syntax:** --raw (no value required)

**Example**

"Urban pedestrian bridge made of hempcrete and rope --raw"

**When to Use It**

Useful when testing material ideas, functional representations, or when one needs to reduce MidJourney's stylistic influence for clearer conceptual fidelity.

### *--tile: Generating Seamless Patterns*

The --tile parameter enables the generation of seamlessly repeatable images, useful for creating patterns, textures, façade systems, or environmental wraps.

- **Syntax:** --tile (no value required)

**Example**

"Biomorphic lattice skin with mossy texture --tile"

**When to Use It**

Best for generating repetitive design systems, tiling wallpapers, or continuous architectural screens and fabrics.

### *--sref: Style Reference*

The --sref parameter allows you to apply the style of a reference image—such as its color palette, lighting, brushwork, or texture—to a new prompt. It functions as a kind of aesthetic transfer, enabling the synthesis of content and external style.

- **Syntax:** --sref [image URL or uploaded image]

**Example**

"A neofuturist opera house by the sea --sref [image URL]"

**When to Use It**

When designers wish to merge formal ideas with a specific visual atmosphere, often for visual consistency across projects or outputs. Crucial for architectural storytelling and brand identity development.

### *--oref: Omni Reference (V7+)*

Introduced in Version 7, the --oref parameter replaces earlier character reference functions and allows for a more generalized reference integration. It can incorporate form, pose, proportion, texture, or identity from an image into the new composition.

- **Syntax:** --oref [image]

**Example**

"Interior view of a suspended meditation chamber --oref [image]"

**When to Use It**

Highly useful when you want to preserve a spatial or formal essence across prompts, such as continuity of a structural system or repeating elements in a design series.

### *--iw: Image Weight*

The --iw parameter controls how much influence an input image has when used alongside text. It determines the balance between visual and linguistic guidance.

- **Syntax:** --iw [0.1–2.0]

**Example**

"Hyperdense vertical farm --iw 0.5 [with reference image]"

**When to Use It**

Critical for fine-tuning hybrid prompts. Lower values prioritize text; higher values tilt interpretation toward the visual prompt.

### *--sw: Style Weight*

The --sw parameter controls how strongly the style reference image affects the final result. This is useful when multiple styles are in play or when more subtle stylistic echoes are desired.

- **Syntax:** --sw [0–1000]

**Example**

"Mountain retreat in the style of abstract watercolor --sref [image] --sw 300"

**When to Use It**

To control whether the reference overwhelms or subtly nuances the image. Essential for artistic direction in portfolio and presentation work.

### *--cw: Character Weight (Legacy)*

Previously used to control how strictly a character reference was applied, --cw is now deprecated in favor of --oref. However, it remains functional in earlier versions and helps manage likeness, silhouette, and identity continuity.

- **Syntax:** --cw [0–100]

**When to Use It**

Mostly for those working with earlier model versions or revisiting saved style presets. In architectural terms, it may have been creatively used to preserve the "character" of a design motif or anthropomorphic structure.

### *--profile / --p: Personalization Profile*

The --profile parameter applies a saved personalization model—a kind of user-trained aesthetic identity or visual signature. These profiles are generated from preferred outputs and enable the automation of stylistic coherence across generations.

- **Syntax:** --profile [name] or --p [name]

**Example**

"Modular school campus in arid climate --profile desert-formalism"

**When to Use It**

Ideal for maintaining design consistency in iterative work or applying a recognizable visual identity across a project series or portfolio.

### *--draft: Rapid Low-Cost Prototyping*

The --draft parameter, introduced in Version 7, activates a lightweight rendering mode. It consumes half the GPU time and delivers results approximately 10× faster, though at reduced detail and stylization.

- **Syntax:** --draft

**Example**

"Early-stage campus masterplan --draft"

**When to Use It**

Perfect for ideation sessions, real-time collaboration, or when computational budget is limited. Allows for sketch-like image testing before committing to high-fidelity runs.

### *--fast: GPU-Powered Speed Mode*

This mode uses GPU processing to accelerate image generation. It offers standard performance and is the default setting unless changed.

- **Syntax:** --fast

**When to Use It**

General-purpose rendering. Best used when visual fidelity is important and time is a factor.

### *--relax: Queue-Friendly, No GPU Cost*

This mode allows unlimited rendering without consuming GPU minutes, but outputs are generated more slowly and processed in shared queues.

- **Syntax:** --relax
- **Availability:** Only for Pro and Mega users.

**When to Use It**

Ideal for batch generation overnight, non-urgent outputs, or background rendering during workshops and teaching sessions.

### *--turbo: Maximum Speed, Lower Detail*

An experimental mode for ultra-fast generation. It sacrifices fine detail and nuance in favor of speed, useful when quick drafts are prioritized over rendering fidelity.

- **Syntax:** --turbo

**When to Use It**

Early conceptual work, thumbnail sketching, or generating prompt variations en masse.

### *--niji: Anime / Stylized Aesthetic Model*

Activates the Niji model, optimized for anime, manga, and stylized illustrative outputs. It overrides standard MidJourney rendering models with one designed specifically for Eastern visual traditions.

- **Syntax:** --niji

#### When to Use It

For working with visual languages outside architectural realism—useful in narrative environments, interactive storytelling, and speculative design.

### *--public / --stealth: Visibility Controls*

These parameters govern whether your generated images are publicly visible on the MidJourney gallery.

- **Syntax:**
  - --public: Makes the image visible to others.
  - --stealth: Keeps image private (Pro and Mega tiers only).

#### When to Use It

--stealth is essential for private research, competition entries, or proprietary project development, while --public may be leveraged for community feedback or visibility.

# Chapter 14

# Video Generation on Midjourney

## --motion: Control Subject and Camera Movement

The --motion parameter determines the intensity of movement within the generated video clip. It governs how dynamic the animation feels, balancing between subtle ambient motion and dramatic cinematic shifts.

- **Syntax:** --motion low or --motion high

**Example**

"A modular housing complex breathing with light and shadow --motion high"

- --motion low: Produces slower, more atmospheric motion—ideal for meditative or realistic animations.
- --motion high: Introduces both camera and object movement for a more dramatic effect.

**When to Use It**

To simulate lived experience, experiment with temporal perception, or animate narrative shifts in space. Particularly compelling in immersive design reviews or exhibitions.

## --loop: Seamless Motion Cycles

The --loop parameter ensures that the generated video begins and ends with nearly identical frames, creating a visually seamless animation loop. This is especially useful for background animations, architectural mood boards, or exhibition visuals.

- **Syntax:** --loop

DOI: 10.1201/9781003637691-16

**Example**

"A kinetic glass pavilion shimmering in the wind --loop"

**When to Use It**

Ideal for social media displays, digital installations, and motion graphics where continuous playback is desired.

**Figure 34.** A video generated from a rendered image. A sequence of 3 screenshots were taken to show the progress of frames in the video.

## --end: Define Final Frame via Image Reference

The --end parameter allows the designer to define a specific ending frame for the video by linking to a MidJourney image. The model will then interpolate a motion sequence that leads from the starting image to the selected endpoint.

- **Syntax:** --end [Job ID or Image URL]

**Example**

"Futurist urban skyline at dawn –end [image URL]" (Fig. 34)

**When to Use It**

Enables the creation of narrative arcs or transformation sequences—e.g., day-to-night transitions, morphological growth, or spatial evolution.

# Chapter 15

# Midjourney Prompt Parameters Overview

| Parameters | What it does |
|---|---|
| *Core Prompt Parameters* | |
| Aspect Ratio (--ar) | Defines image width-to-height ratio. |
| Version (--v) | Selects the MidJourney model version. |
| Quality (--q) | Controls rendering detail and GPU processing time. |
| Stylize (--s) | Controls the degree of artistic abstraction. |
| Seed (--seed) | Sets random seed for reproducibility. |
| Chaos (--chaos / --c) | Increases randomness and diversity in output. |
| Repeat (--repeat / --r) | Generates multiple images from one prompt. |
| Weird (--weird / --w) | Introduces experimental, quirky aesthetic. |
| Stop (--stop) | Terminates generation early (for sketch-like images). |
| Raw Mode (--raw) | Disables aesthetic filtering for literal output. |
| Tile (--tile) | Creates seamless, repeating patterns. |
| *Reference and Style Parameters* | |
| Image Weight (--iw): | Balances influence of image prompts. |
| Style Reference (--sref): | Applies visual style of reference image. |
| Omni Reference (--oref | Integrates form/style/shape from reference (V7+). |
| Style Weight (--sw): | Controls intensity of style influence. |
| Character Weight (--cw): | Legacy weight for character likeness (deprecated). |
| Profile (--profile / --p): | Applies a saved aesthetic profile to prompt. |
| *Workflow and Mode Parameters* | |
| Draft Mode (--draft): | Generates fast, low-cost image drafts. |
| Fast Mode (--fast): | Faster rendering, consumes GPU time. |
| Relax Mode (--relax): | Slower, non-consuming mode for Pro users. |

DOI: 10.1201/9781003637691-17

| | |
|---|---|
| Turbo Mode (--turbo): | Very fast image generation, lower detail. |
| Niji Mode (--niji): | Anime/Eastern aesthetics model. |
| Public (--public): | Publishes output to public feed. |
| Stealth (--stealth): | Keeps output private (Pro/Mega only). |
| No (Negative Prompting) (--no): | Excludes specific elements from image. |
| ***Workflow and Mode Parameters*** | |
| Motion Level (--motion low/ high): | Controls intensity of subject/camera movement. |
| Loop (--loop): | Creates seamless looped video. |
| End Frame (--end [URL]): | Designates a final frame for the video. |
| ***Discord Commands*** | |
| /imagine (): | Main image generation command. |
| /blend (): | Combines multiple images into one. |
| /describe (): | Converts an image into prompt suggestions. |
| /settings (): | Opens user configuration panel. |
| /prefer remix (): | Enables Remix Mode for prompt editing. |
| /prefer suffix (): | Appends suffix to every prompt automatically. |
| /shorten (): | Suggests optimized versions of long prompts. |
| /synonyms (): | Finds alternative lexical terms for prompts. |
| /tune (): | Creates Style Tuners based on prompt history. |
| /list_tuners | Displays saved Style Tuners. |
| /fast / /relax / /turbo (): | Toggles image generation speed modes. |
| /show (): | Regenerates an image using a known Job ID. |
| /info (): | Displays account and job usage details. |

Chapter 16

# Practical Guide to Using COMFY UI in Architecture

## Introduction to Comfy UI

ComfyUI is an open-source, node-based user interface designed for advanced workflows in AI image generation. It provides users with a highly customizable and intuitive environment to create, manipulate, and refine visual outputs generated by deep learning models. Unlike traditional command-line interfaces or pre-configured GUIs, Comfy UI emphasizes flexibility and control, catering to both novice users and experienced practitioners who require fine-grained adjustments for creative or technical projects.

The platform is widely recognized for its ability to visualize complex generative processes through a network of interconnected nodes, each representing a distinct step in the image synthesis pipeline. These nodes allow users to experiment with parameters such as model weights, input data, and post-processing effects, making it a preferred tool for tasks ranging from artistic experimentation to professional design workflows, including architectural visualization (Fig 35).

COMFY UI's primary utility lies in its ability to facilitate experimentation and refinement in AI-driven image creation. The workflow typically involves the following steps:

1. **Node-Based Workflow**: Users build workflows by connecting nodes, each representing an operation such as text-to-image generation, image-to-image refinement, or style application. This modular approach enables iterative experimentation and the ability to trace the creative process visually.
2. **Customization**: Users can fine-tune parameters such as model selection, resolution, noise levels, and style attributes, allowing for precise control over the generated output.

DOI: 10.1201/9781003637691-18

3. **Integration with AI Models**: COMFY UI supports multiple AI models, including Stable Diffusion, offering a platform to leverage pre-trained models while allowing modifications for specific needs.
4. **Visualization and Debugging**: The node-based system enables real-time visualization of intermediate outputs, making it easier to identify and address issues in the workflow.
5. **Applications**: COMFY UI is used extensively in fields such as architecture, game design, film production, and digital art. For architects, it is particularly valuable for creating schematic designs, visualizing concepts, and generating realistic renderings.

This COMFY UI modular emerged as a response to the growing demand for more user-friendly interfaces in the field of AI-driven creative tools. It was developed as an open-source project by a community of engineers, artists, and researchers who identified the need for a versatile and transparent platform for managing complex generative tasks.

- **Origins and Development**: The platform began as an experimental project aimed at simplifying the use of Stable Diffusion models. Early versions focused on providing a graphical interface for non-technical users while retaining advanced features for experts.
- **Milestones**:
  - **2022**: Initial conceptualization and beta release, gaining traction among AI enthusiasts and early adopters.
  - **2023**: Major updates introduced support for multi-model workflows and enhanced visualization capabilities, solidifying its reputation as a leading tool for creative professionals.
  - **2024**: Integration with advanced AI models and expanded customization options, making it a staple in academic and professional contexts.

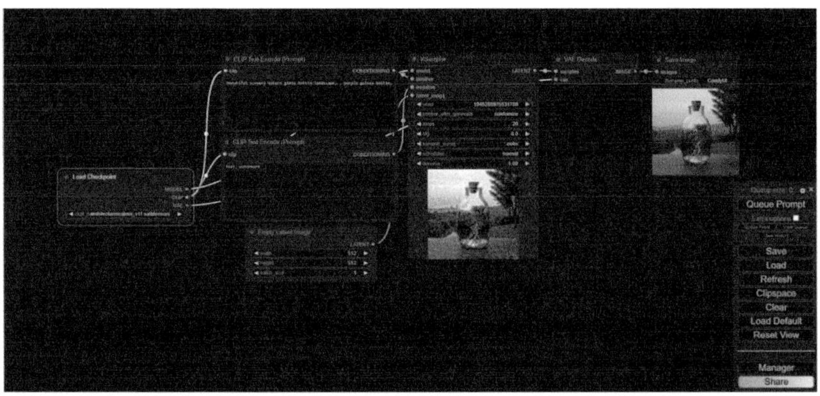


**Figure 35.** The default web interface pipeline of Comfy UI.

Chapter 17

# ComfyUI for Image Generation

## Checkpoints, Prompts, and Sampling Logic

ComfyUI is an advanced, node-based visual environment built explicitly around the logic of latent diffusion models, primarily Stable Diffusion. Unlike conventional text-to-image services, such as MidJourney or DALL-E, ComfyUI provides complete transparency and control over every aspect of the image generation pipeline. Users can directly manipulate diffusion models, conditioning mechanisms, and sampling procedures at the granular level, rendering it especially suitable for architectural workflows where precise spatial and stylistic control are essential.

This chapter provides foundational knowledge essential for understanding ComfyUI's underlying generative logic, its node-based workflows, and the key considerations when designing image-generation pipelines in an architectural context.

### Loading the Base Model (Checkpoints)

A checkpoint, also called a base diffusion model, encapsulates a neural network's trained parameters, derived from extensive datasets (often comprising hundreds of millions of image-caption pairs). These checkpoint files (.safetensors or .ckpt) define the generative "brain" of the pipeline (Fig. 36), encompassing:

- **UNet:** The core denoising architecture responsible for the iterative image refinement process.
- **CLIP Text Encoder:** Encodes text prompts into semantic vectors for conditioning.

DOI: 10.1201/9781003637691-19

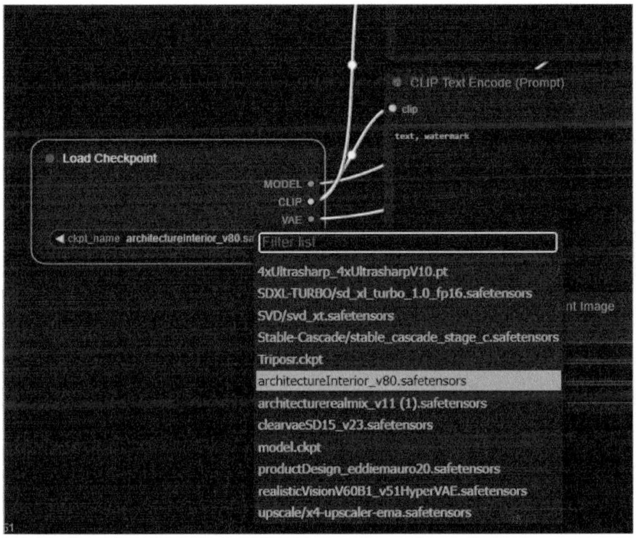


**Figure 36.** The list of pre-trained models to use as checkpoints.

- **VAE (Variational Autoencoder):** Encodes and decodes latent images into recognizable pixel space.

**Node Workflow:**

- **Node:** Load Checkpoint
- **Inputs:** Path to .safetensors or .ckpt
- **Outputs:** Model object (UNet), conditioning modules (CLIP), and latent encoding/decoding module (VAE)

**Critical Technical Considerations:**

- **Model and Conditioning Compatibility:**

Each model variant (e.g., Stable Diffusion v1.5, SDXL, or custom fine-tuned checkpoints) has specific CLIP and VAE architectures. Mixing incompatible components (for instance, using SD1.5 CLIP encoding with an SDXL checkpoint) often results in failed renders, distorted geometry, or nonsensical output.
Always ensure model-encoder compatibility to maintain stable outputs.

## Prompt Injection and Text Conditioning

Text prompts constitute the semantic input guiding the image generation process. The CLIP (Contrastive Language-Image Pretraining) encoder translates plain English descriptions into vector embeddings—numerical

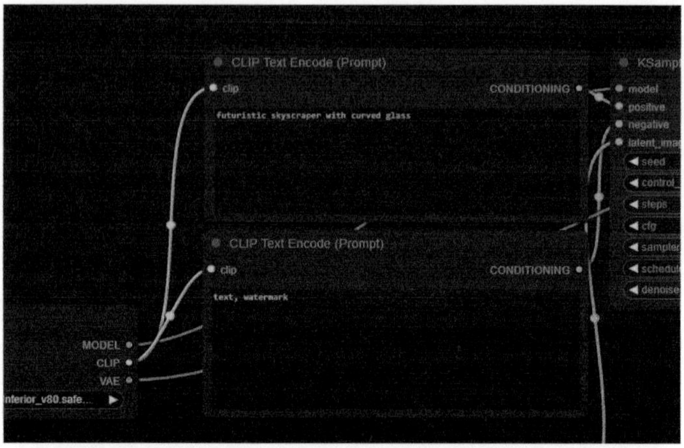


**Figure 37.** Text encoder- Positive and Negative prompt.

representations of meaning that the diffusion model can interpret and operationalize (Fig. 37).

**Node Workflow and Example:**

- **Node:** CLIPTextEncode
- **Input:** Textual description of desired image
- **Output:** Vector embedding (conditioning tensor)

**Architectural Example:**

Prompt: *"A timber library on a hilltop at sunset, minimalist architecture"* CLIP Conditioning Output: Vector embedding directing latent-space generation toward architectural specificity (timber, minimalist style, hillside location).

**Negative Prompts:**

Negative prompts provide semantic vectors indicating features to exclude (e.g., "blurry," "distorted," "poorly detailed"), significantly improving architectural clarity and spatial accuracy.

- **Workflow:** Separate CLIPTextEncode node → negative conditioning input of sampler node.
- **Impact:** Strongly recommended for architectural precision to suppress visual noise or unwanted stylistic artifacts.

**Latent Image Initialization**

Before the diffusion process begins, ComfyUI initializes a latent tensor—a low-dimensional noise representation that the model progressively refines into a coherent image.

**Node and Parameters:**

- **Node:** EmptyLatentImage
- **Critical Parameters:**
  - o **Resolution:** Typically square or architectural aspect ratios (512×512, 768×1024, etc.)
  - o **Batch Size:** Determines how many images generate simultaneously.
  - o **Seed:** Random number initializing noise state; ensures repeatability or intentional variation.

**Architectural Best Practice:**

Changing only the seed with a fixed prompt and checkpoint yields minor variations while preserving spatial consistency—ideal for design iteration.

**Sampling: The Generative Core**

The heart of the diffusion process is iterative denoising, executed by specialized sampler nodes (KSampler and advanced variants like KSamplerAdvanced). The sampler progressively refines the latent image, guided by prompt conditioning vectors and noise schedules.

**Key Sampling Parameters:**

At the heart of any diffusion-based image generation in ComfyUI lies the KSampler node—an algorithmic engine that defines how noise is iteratively transformed into coherent architectural imagery. Unlike traditional rendering engines, which simulate geometry, material reflectance, and physical light transport, the KSampler simulates a *plausibility trajectory* within a pre-trained generative manifold. That is, it translates a latent random field into a resolved visual output, conditioned by prompt, structure, or guidance maps (Fig. 38).

**Table 4.** Sampling parameters of the K sampler.

| **Parameter** | **Architectural Impact** | **Optimal Range (Architectural Context)** |
|---|---|---|
| **Sampling Steps** | Determines image clarity vs. render time | 25–40 (for architectural detail) |
| **CFG Scale** | Balances prompt fidelity and generative freedom | 7.0–9.0 (for precise spatial adherence) |
| **Sampler Algorithm** | Tradeoff between sharpness and coherence | DPM++ 2M Karras (optimal for architecture) |
| **Denoising Strength** | Degree to adhere to an initial input (image-to-image pipeline) | 0.3–0.6 (for guided architectural adjustments) |
| **Seed** | Random numbers to generate iterations | 0- 99999999999 |

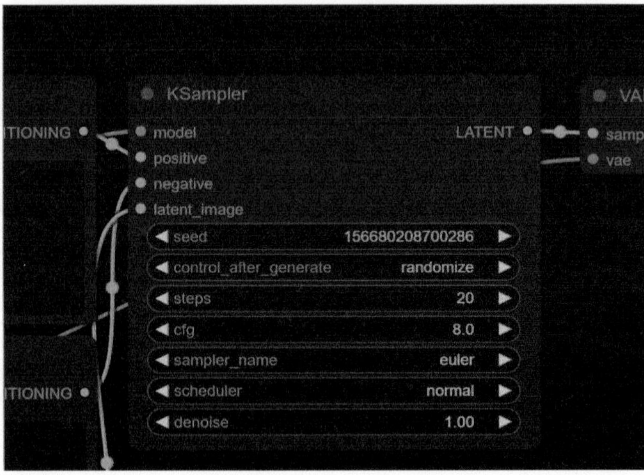


**Figure 38.** A screenshot of the (Regular not advanced) Ksampler.

The behavior of this translation is modulated through several key parameters:

### Sampling Steps

The step count determines how many iterations the model uses to denoise the latent space and converge toward the final image.

- **Low step counts (2–6)**: These yield fast results but often remain blurry or underdeveloped—useful for rapid ideation or mood studies.
- **Mid to high step counts (10–50)**: As seen in the comparison images, increasing steps introduces architectural detail, corrects spatial proportions, and sharpens textures.
- **Very high steps (100+)**: Rarely needed, but useful for extremely complex or high-resolution prompts when using models with larger receptive fields.

The architectural analogy would be sketching: early strokes define mood, but more passes give material, structure, and articulation (Fig. 39).

### CFG Scale (cfg) — Classifier-Free Guidance

This governs how strictly the image adheres to the prompt text.

- **Low CFG (1.0–4.0)**: The model explores broader interpretations, yielding poetic, dream-like results. In the provided grid, low-CFG images remained visually soft but often strayed semantically.
- **Medium CFG (6.0–8.0)**: This range achieves balance—architectural prompts are respected while still allowing for generative creativity.

**Figure 39.** This figure explains how CFG Scale and Sampling Steps affect the AI's response to a prompt. The CFG Scale controls how closely the AI follows your instructions: a low CFG (1.0) gives the AI more freedom, leading to abstract or random outputs, while a high CFG (10.0) forces the AI to stick closely to the design brief, producing clearer and more accurate results. Sampling Steps determine how many refinement passes the AI makes—fewer steps result in rough, blurry images, while higher steps (10–12) produce more detailed and polished visuals. Together, these two settings allow you to fine-tune between fast creative sketches and high-quality architectural visuals. (Undale, 2025)

- **High CFG (10.0–12.0)**: Forces the model to rigidly follow the prompt, which can produce sharp but sometimes grotesque or collapsed results, especially if the prompt is over-specified or ill-structured.

In architectural terms, think of CFG as the difference between a poetic brief ("a serene forest retreat") and a code specification ("a two-storey timber-clad volume with 4m cantilever").

### Denoise Strength

This controls how much of the original latent noise is preserved versus transformed during generation (Fig. 40).

- **Lower values (0.5–0.7)**: Preserve more of the original noise. These are useful for inpainting, interpolation, or retaining structure from a previous image.
- **Higher values (0.9–1.0)**: Allow the model to regenerate the image from near-scratch. In the example sheet, increasing denoise produced progressively sharper, richer images, but also greater variability across seeds.

Used wisely, this parameter can blend structure preservation with stylistic refresh—ideal for evolving massing studies while maintaining design logic.

### Seed

The seed controls the pseudo-random starting point of the noise field. Keeping the same seed with different CFGs, samplers, or prompts allows for controlled comparison. Changing the seed introduces variation—useful when exploring multiple formal options from a single conceptual prompt.

In practice, designers often "lock" a seed to stabilize form during stylistic variation, or iterate seeds to discover unexpected compositions

### Sampler Type (sampler_name)

The sampler algorithm defines how the latent noise field is denoised over time. Different samplers represent different mathematical methods of traversing the diffusion process (Fig. 41).

- **Euler / Euler A**: Fast, general-purpose, good for stylistic sketches.
- **DPM++ 2M / DPM++ SDE**: More stable, especially in high-resolution architectural generation. They reduce noise artifacts while preserving detail.
- **UniPC, LCM, DDIM**: Each has different trade-offs between speed, sharpness, and coherence.

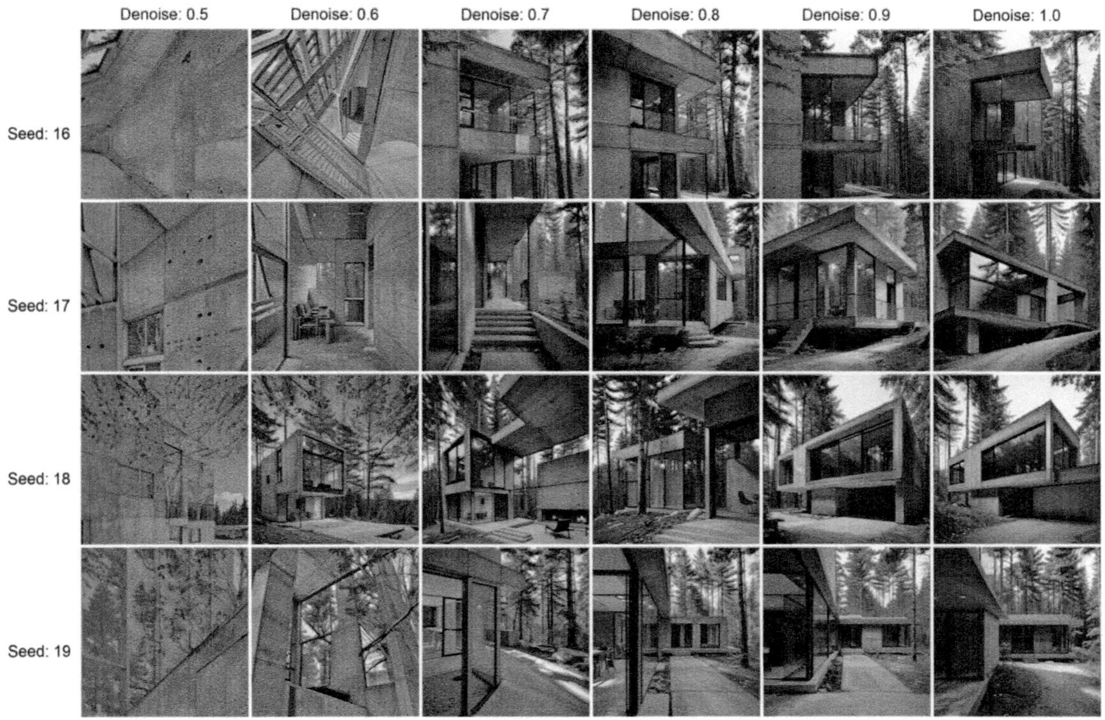


**Figure 40.** This figure shows how changing the Denoise Strength affects the AI's ability to modify or preserve an image. At low values (0.5–0.6), the images stay very close to the original, with only small changes in textures or lighting. As the value increases to 0.7–0.8, the AI starts to suggest new design elements—such as different facade details or window arrangements—while still respecting the overall structure. At high values (0.9–1.0), the AI takes more control and reimagines the design entirely, introducing new forms, materials, or environmental features. Denoise Strength, therefore, acts as a slider between design refinement and creative exploration, allowing architects to decide how much influence the AI should have on the output. (Undale, 2025)

**Figure 41.** Here, the outputs from different Model Checkpoints are compared, showing how each model brings its own style and visual character. Juggernaut_aftermath and RealisticVision models focus on photorealistic, detailed renderings—perfect for realistic architectural visualizations. OpenDalleV1.1, on the other hand, gives more abstract and less detailed results, useful for early concept studies. FantasyWorld_v10 adds surreal and exaggerated elements, creating more imaginative visuals. Toonyou_beta6 stylizes the image into a cartoon-like aesthetic. Choosing the right model is crucial, as it determines whether your output looks realistic, conceptual, fantastical, or stylized, depending on your design goals (Undale, 2025).

Changing changing samplers on the same prompt and seed leads to vastly different results—from clean, orthogonal elevations to surreal, distorted spaces. The choice of sampler is a compositional decision—akin to choosing between watercolor, oil paint, or pencil.

**Decoding the Latent to Image**

Post-sampling, the latent representation is still abstract. To visualize it, a Variational Autoencoder (VAE) decodes this latent tensor back into RGB pixel space.

- **Node:** VAE Decode
- **Critical Requirement:** Must match the VAE used during checkpoint training; mismatch results in corrupted or blank output images.

**Architectural Impact:**

Ensuring the correct VAE decoder is essential for accurately reproducing spatial proportions, lighting conditions, and material textures encoded within the model.

**Saving or Previewing the Output**

ComfyUI provides multiple nodes to output the resulting imagery for direct use, visualization, or iterative design review.

- **SaveImage Node:** Exports generated images directly to disk; allows specification of naming conventions, format (PNG, JPG), and output directory.
- **PreviewImage Node:** Displays immediate visual feedback within ComfyUI's interface, invaluable for rapid iteration and real-time workflow adjustments.
- **ImageViewer Node:** Inline node preview within the node graph; helps quickly verify intermediate steps and debugging purposes. Additional Clarifications:
- **Control over Checkpoint Quality:**

Not all checkpoints are created equal; for architecture, checkpoints trained specifically on built-environment datasets produce superior spatial and stylistic consistency.

**Prompt Engineering in Architectural Context:**

Architectural prompts require precision in specifying materials, atmospheric conditions, spatial relationships, and formal characteristics. Ambiguous or overly abstract prompts typically yield less useful outcomes.

- **Batch Generation and Iterative Refinement:**

Employing batch rendering with varying seeds or minor parameter tweaks helps identify stable spatial and stylistic characteristics, ensuring robust architectural imagery.

Mastering ComfyUI requires a nuanced understanding of checkpoints, textual conditioning, latent operations, and sampling strategies. Architectural image generation, distinct from artistic or illustrative workflows, emphasizes coherence, structural clarity, and material realism (Fig. 42).

The subsequent chapters build upon this foundational pipeline by introducing more advanced latent conditioning techniques, visual control mechanisms, and precision-enhancing strategies specifically developed for architectural applications.

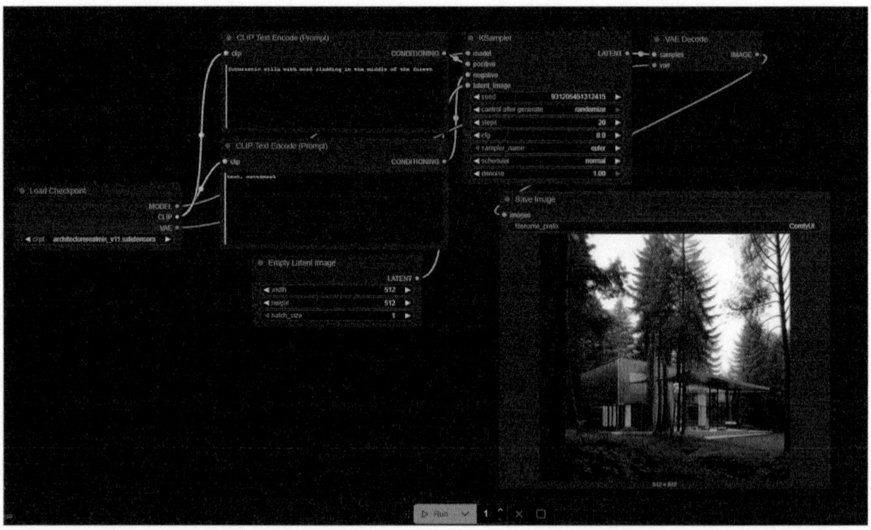


**Figure 42.** Basic pipeline to produce an architectural output on ComfyUI.

# Chapter 18

# Latent Conditioning and ControlNet

## Precision Through Visual Guides

Generative diffusion models, while exceptionally capable at synthesizing images from textual prompts alone, inherently tend toward stylistic and structural ambiguity. For architectural applications—where precise spatial logic, scale accuracy, and formal clarity are paramount—relying purely on text-based prompts often proves insufficient. To mitigate this limitation, latent conditioning techniques can explicitly guide the generative process using external visual data.

Within ComfyUI, the most sophisticated and robust method for latent conditioning is ControlNet, a neural network module specifically developed to integrate visual cues—such as line drawings, depth maps, or segmentation masks—into the diffusion process. By conditioning diffusion models on external spatial information, architects can significantly enhance spatial coherence, reduce unwanted generative hallucination, and retain essential stylistic flexibility.

## Understanding ControlNet: Principles and Operation

ControlNet is an auxiliary neural network designed to run in parallel with a primary diffusion model (e.g., Stable Diffusion). Rather than directly generating images, it serves as a structured conditioning mechanism, guiding the latent diffusion process via intermediate feature maps derived from externally provided visual inputs.

DOI: 10.1201/9781003637691-20

**Fundamental Components of ControlNet within ComfyUI:**

- **ControlNetLoader:**

Loads a specific, pretrained ControlNet variant compatible with the chosen feature extraction method (e.g., Canny, Depth, Lineart).

- **Preprocessors:**

Convert user-provided images (sketches, renders, diagrams) into standardized structural feature maps. Examples include:

  - **Canny edge detection:** Extracts high-contrast edges from sketches.
  - **Midas Depth estimation:** Estimates relative depth from grayscale renders or photos.
  - **MLSD line detection:** Captures structural straight lines for geometric precision.
  - **Lineart detection:** Extracts simplified vector-like edges, ideal for clean CAD or digital linework.

- **ControlNetApply:**

Integrates the feature map produced by the preprocessor into the latent sampling process, constraining generative outputs to the provided structural logic.

## Standard ComfyUI Node Workflow for ControlNet

A basic ControlNet pipeline within ComfyUI typically follows a sequential node graph structure:

[Input Image] → [Preprocessor] → [ControlNetLoader] → [ControlNetApply] → [KSampler] (Fig. 43).

**Detailed Architectural Functionality of Each Node:**

- **Input Image Node:**

Accepts original architectural imagery—such as sketches, renders, CAD linework, or volumetric masks.

- **Preprocessor Node:**

Processes input images into latent-compatible structural feature maps. Critical preprocessing modes include:

  - Canny: For sketches and rough massing diagrams.
  - MidasDepth: For depth-aware facade and interior studies.

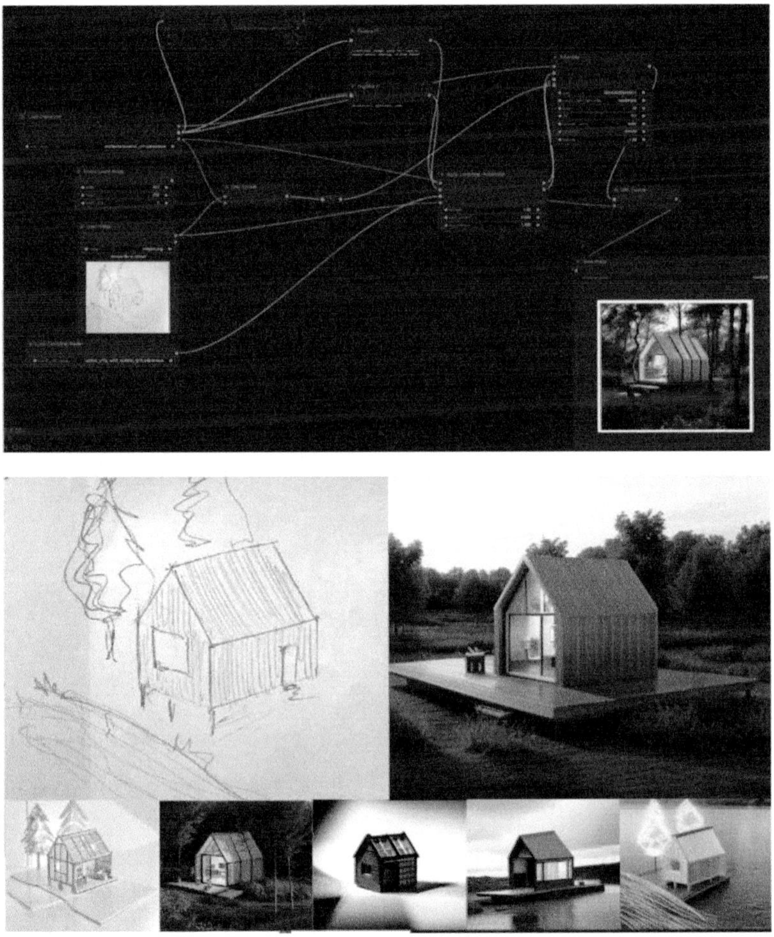

**Figure 43.** A result of from sketch to render (and its iterations) by one of the students at Brno University of Technology (Jan Bilek, 2024).

- MLSD: For structured architectural drawings and precise geometries.
- LineartRealistic: For refined vector-like line drawings from CAD or vector sources.

- **ControlNetLoader Node:**

Loads the pretrained neural network corresponding exactly to the chosen preprocessor. Mismatches here cause generative instability or structural failures.

- **ControlNetApply Node:**

Injects conditioning data directly into the latent diffusion model, preserving the architectural integrity of initial inputs while allowing stylistic flexibility.

## Practical Architectural Applications of ControlNet

a. **Sketch-Constrained Massing Studies**

Quickly explore schematic form variations guided by initial sketches or silhouettes, maintaining proportional coherence and massing logic.

- **Preprocessor:** Canny edge detection
- **ControlNet variant:** control_v11p_sd15_canny
- **Typical Usage:** Early design stages, urban massing explorations, iterative volumetric studies.

b. **Depth-Driven Facade Development**

Precisely maintain facade depth, layer relationships, and spatial hierarchy via depth maps derived from either renders or estimated grayscale images.

- **Preprocessor:** Midas Depth
- **ControlNet variant:** control_v11f1p_sd15_depth
- **Typical Usage:** Detailed facade refinement, interior spatial depth studies, and volumetric sectioning.

c. **Structural Linework Integration**

Use structured architectural drawings—plans, sections, elevations—as conditioning inputs to rigorously control generative outputs.

- **Preprocessor:** LineartRealistic or MLSD
- **ControlNet variant:** control_v11p_sd15_lineart or control_v11p_sd15_mlsd
- **Typical Usage:** Plan-to-elevation conversions, rigorous structural or geometric constraints, formal exploration based on precise CAD data.

## Adjusting Conditioning Strength and Temporal Control

The ControlNetApply node includes two critical parameters, essential for nuanced architectural control:

- **Control Weight (range: 0.0–2.0):**

Dictates how strongly the model adheres to the input structural guide.

- o Architectural Recommendation: 0.8–1.4

  - Below 0.8 risks insufficient adherence, above 1.4 risks rigidity and loss of generative exploration.
- **Start/End Percent (range: 0.0–1.0):**

Defines at what stages of latent denoising the ControlNet conditioning is active.

  - Example Architectural Setting:
    - Start: 0.0, End: 0.8 allows early-stage structure definition with late-stage stylistic flexibility.

These parameters enable architects to strike an optimal balance between strict structural accuracy and necessary generative flexibility, ensuring that the resulting imagery remains both faithful and innovative.

## Latent Conditioning versus Pixel Conditioning: A Critical Distinction

ControlNet operates explicitly in the latent space, not the pixel space:

- Input images do not directly overlay onto or composite into the final render.
- Instead, their structural information (edges, depth cues, vectors) is translated into latent feature maps, guiding—but not replacing—the generative process.
- Thus, architectural fidelity is preserved structurally, yet stylistic, textural, and atmospheric variation remains dynamic and adaptable through prompts and additional conditioning mechanisms.

This latent-level distinction is crucial for understanding the nature and effectiveness of ControlNet conditioning in architectural applications.

## Architectural Best Practices for ControlNet Integration

- **Maintain consistent aspect ratios** between ControlNet input images and the latent generation tensor to avoid unintended deformation or proportion distortion.
- **Limit the number of simultaneous ControlNet modules:** Excessive stacking (beyond two parallel modules) generally reduces the clarity of architectural conditioning. Only combine complementary modes (e.g., Depth + Lineart).

- **Adjust CFG scale accordingly:**

Higher CFG scales (> 9) may override or reduce the structural influence of ControlNet. Optimal CFG range for strong architectural ControlNet usage is typically 6–8.

- **Integrate complementary conditioning nodes:**

IPAdapter or ReferenceOnly nodes, discussed in later chapters, complement ControlNet's structural guidance by providing stylistic coherence.

Known Limitations and Potential Risks

- **Over-conditioning (weights > 1.5):**

May produce overly rigid, robotic forms, lacking architectural nuance or generative richness.

- **Preprocessor mismatch:**

Using incompatible preprocessor and ControlNet model pairs (e.g., MidasDepth image with Canny model) can result in failed or nonsensical outputs.

- **Resolution mismatch:**

Structural fidelity is severely compromised if ControlNet input image resolution significantly differs from latent generation dimensions.

- **Semantic prompt conflicts:**

Highly stylistic or inconsistent prompts can cause confusion within the latent model, resulting in structural drift or failure, even with ControlNet present.

## Conclusion

ControlNet introduces an unprecedented degree of spatial accuracy and structural logic into the inherently stochastic domain of latent diffusion image generation. Architects leveraging ComfyUI with ControlNet gain powerful tools for iterative design exploration, schematic validation, and stylistically flexible yet structurally coherent architectural visualization.

# Chapter 19

# Architectural Animation in ComfyUI

## Video Generation and Consistency Control

### Introduction: Generative Animation as an Architectural Tool

ComfyUI has evolved from a still-image generator into a sophisticated platform for architectural animation, enabling designers to create cinematic sequences, spatial walkthroughs, and temporal design studies without traditional 3D geometry. By leveraging latent-space coherence, sequential conditioning, and temporal control mechanisms, architects simulate motion, transformation, and environmental dynamics directly from generative workflows. This chapter demystifies video generation in ComfyUI, emphasizing techniques for achieving structural consistency and cinematic fidelity (Fig. 44).

### Core Principles of Architectural Animation

*The Frame-by-Frame Paradigm*

ComfyUI generates video through discrete image sequences, not real-time diffusion. Each frame is individually synthesized, then compiled into motion. Key challenges include:

- **Temporal Consistency**: Avoiding flicker, object shifts, or noise instability.

DOI: 10.1201/9781003637691-21

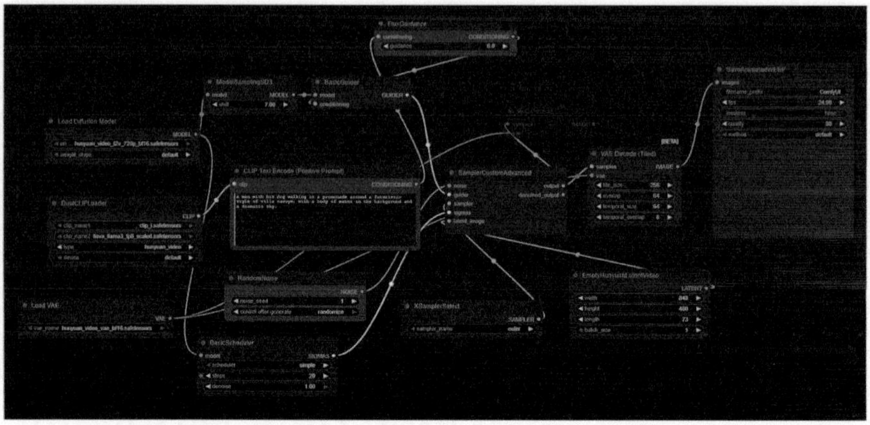

**Figure 44.** Video creation workflow with a Hunyuan model.

- **Controlled Transformation**: Precisely governing changes in form, material, or perspective.
- **Resource Optimization**: Balancing VRAM limits with output quality.
**Four Animation Strategies**

| Method | Mechanism | Architectural Use Case |
|---|---|---|
| **Latent Interpolation** | Blending noise states between images | Morphing façade typologies |
| **Prompt Interpolation** | Gradual CLIP embedding shifts | Material transitions (brick → glass) |
| **Camera Simulation** | Cropping/translating latent grids | Sectional walkthroughs, detail zooms |
| **ControlNet Anchoring** | External guides (depth/edges) per frame | Stabilizing structural elements |

## Temporal Consistency Techniques

### A. Latent Interpolation (Design Morphing)

**Workflow**:

1. Generate start/end images (e.g., "Gothic cathedral" → "Modernist museum").
2. Use LatentInterpolator to create intermediate states (e.g., 30 frames).
3. Decode latents → compile frames via VideoHelper or FFmpeg.

**Best Practices**:

- Freeze seed and CFG (e.g., seed=42, cfg=7) to minimize noise divergence.
- Use VAE Decode Tiled with temporal overlap for smoother blends.

### B. Prompt Interpolation (Dynamic Styling)

**Tools**: Prompt Scheduler nodes or custom Python scripts.
**Example**:

Frame 1: "Concrete brutalist tower at dawn"

Frame 24: "Glazed parametric tower at noon"

**Pro Tip**: Interpolate CLIP embeddings, not raw text, for subtler transitions.

### C. Camera Motion Simulation

**Techniques**:

- **High-Res Base Render** (e.g., 2048×3072) → LatentCrop/ LatentTranslate per frame.
- **Zoom Effects**: LatentZoom + re-decoding to emulate dolly shots.

**Architectural Application**:

*Animate a zoom from streetscape scale to brickwork details, revealing material texture.*

### D. ControlNet Stabilization

**Workflow**:

1. Precompute edge/depth/segment maps for all frames (e.g., via Blender or ComfyUI).
2. Load sequence with LoopingLoader → inject into each frame's generation.

**Critical for**:

- Preserving window mullions, stair profiles, or grid structures.
- Avoiding "hallucinated" elements in sequential views.

## Native Video Models in ComfyUI (2024-2025)

## Integrated Architect-Driven Pipelines

| Model | Key Features | VRAM | Architectural Edge |
|---|---|---|---|
| **Hunyuan Video** | Cinematic lighting, spatial coherence | 16GB+ | Mood studies, speculative walkthroughs |
| **Wan VACE 2.2** | First-last frame interpolation, control | 16GB+ | Façade evolution, urban phasing |
| **PixVerse (API)** | Dynamic motion, stylized transitions | API | Concept storyboards |
| **Luma (API)** | Camera path elegance | API | Courtyard fly-throughs, site scans |

Hunyuan Video Workflow Example

*Prompt*: "Limestone gallery, raking light, slow pan across vaulted ceilings"

**Wan VACE for Design Transformation**

- **Input**: First frame (sketch), last frame (final design).
- **Output**: 48-frame interpolation with ControlNet depth consistency.
- **Use Case**: Visualize construction sequencing from scaffold to finished structure.

**Production Pipeline: From Frames to Video**

**Export Workflow**

1. **Frame Generation**: Output PNG sequence (e.g., frame_001.png, frame_002.png).
2. **Compilation**:
   - **ComfyUI's Video Helper**: Drag/drop frame folder → set FPS → render MP4.
   - **FFmpeg Command**:

ffmpeg -framerate 12 -i frame_%03d.png -c:v libx264 -pix_fmt yuv420p output.mp4

**Optimization Checklist**

- Test at 12 FPS → final render at 24 FPS.
- Limit sequences to 48 frames for iterative testing.
- Use Low VRAM Mode for >720p resolutions.

**Architectural Applications**

**Case Studies**

1. **Daylight Simulation**:
   - *Method*: Prompt interpolation shifting shadow angles.
   - *Prompt Flow*: "9 AM sharp shadows" → "3 PM soft shadows"
2. **Urban Phasing**:
   - *Tool*: Wan VACE + segmented maps.
   - *Output*: Neighborhood evolution over 50 years.
3. **Structural Morphology**:
   - *Technique*: Latent interpolation between massing models.

Avoid These Pitfalls

- **Prompt Drift**: Unplanned stylistic shifts mid-sequence (fix: freeze CFG/seed).

- **Jitter**: Inconsistent edges (solution: pre-render ControlNet guides at fixed resolution).
- **VRAM Crash**: Use --medvram flag or tile large renders.

**Animation as a Design Language**

ComfyUI redefines architectural visualization by treating the latent space as a temporal canvas. Through controlled interpolation, guided consistency, and native video models, architects gain a toolkit for:

- **Temporal Storytelling**: Visualizing phased construction or adaptive reuse.
- **Immersive Experience**: Generating walkthroughs without 3D modeling overhead.
- **Generative Experimentation**: Rapidly testing design alternatives in motion.

The future lies in hybrid workflows—e.g., ComfyUI-generated keyframes enhanced by Runway Gen-4 for photorealism—blending generative speed with cinematic polish.

# Chapter 20

# Image Preprocessing

## Resizing, Scaling, and Alignment in the Latent Pipeline

Architectural rendering with AI demands more than aesthetic generation; it requires geometric and spatial precision. In ComfyUI, this begins not with the prompt, but with the image and latent preparation. Whether conditioning on a sketch, applying depth maps, or using image-to-image pipelines, the dimensions and proportions of input images must be aligned with the target output to preserve structural coherence and avoid unintended distortions (Fig. 45).

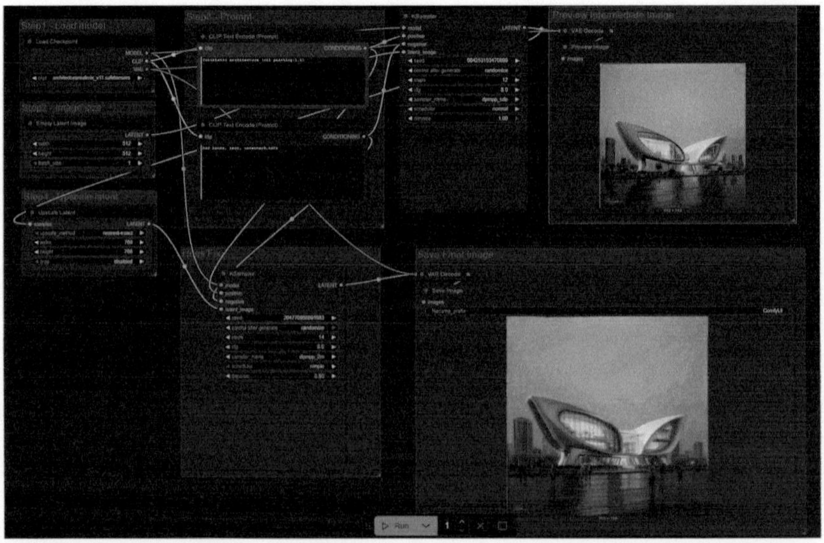

**Figure 45.** Resizing workflow, which will also increase the details by AI generating little details to fill in new pixels.

DOI: 10.1201/9781003637691-22

This chapter outlines how ComfyUI handles image resizing, latent grid scaling, and input-output alignment—fundamentals often overlooked yet essential for architectural control.

## Pixel Space vs. Latent Space

Before diving into resizing mechanics, it's essential to distinguish two domains:

- **Pixel Space**: The actual resolution of input/output images (e.g., 1024×1536 PNG).
- **Latent Space**: The compressed tensor representation where generation happens (typically 1/8 of pixel dimensions, e.g., 128×192 for SD1.5).

All resizing operations must consider both domains. Mismatches—such as feeding a 1024×768 sketch into a 768×1024 latent pipeline—can result in hallucinated proportions, stretched geometry, or cutoff details.

## Loading and Resizing Input Images

**Node**: LoadImage

This loads the initial conditioning image (sketch, mask, depth map). It preserves the native pixel size unless explicitly resized downstream.

**Node: ResizeImage**

Resizes the image to a specified width and height. Options include:

- Keep aspect ratio
- Force dimensions (can distort)
- Center crop and pad

**Best Practice**: For architectural control, resize all inputs to match the generation resolution (e.g., 1024×1536) before sending to the encoder or ControlNet preprocessor.

## Latent Scaling

Some operations act on the latent tensor directly—before decoding it to an image.

Node: ScaleLatent

This rescales the latent grid itself, useful when:

- Changing resolution after generation

- Applying camera zoom effects
- Preparing for sequential generation (video, tiling)

However, since latent space does not preserve perfect geometric ratios, latent scaling is approximate, not pixel-accurate.

## Cropping and Alignment

**Node**: CropImage

Used when a specific region of an image is needed—for example, zooming into a façade detail or removing borders from a scanned sketch.

**Node: CenterCropLatent**

Crops the latent grid at the center, useful for symmetrical massing or framing.

Tip: Always check the final resolution post-crop. Any mismatch between latent and pixel space downstream can cause decoding artifacts or empty outputs.

## Aligning ControlNet and Output

When using ControlNet, the conditioning image and latent image must match resolution and aspect ratio.

Mismatch leads to:

- Misaligned guides
- Off-center compositions
- Structural compression/stretching

Always ensure that:

- The sketch or depth image is resized via ResizeImage
- The generation pipeline (via EmptyLatentImage) is initialized with the same dimensions

## Advanced Use: Aspect Ratio Switching

Changing aspect ratios allows for targeted architectural output:

- --ar 2:3: Portraits, towers, interiors
- --ar 3:2: Landscape, site views, urban plans
- --ar 1:1: Elevations, diagrams

In ComfyUI, this is controlled via the dimensions passed to EmptyLatentImage and ResizeImage. No need for prompt modifiers—aspect control is fully manual.

## Use Case: Façade Iteration with Cropped Sketch

Objective: Use a horizontal sketch of a building façade and explore material variations.

Steps:

1. Load sketch via LoadImage (e.g., 2400×800)
2. Crop to central section via CropImage (e.g., 1600×800)
3. Resize to match generation resolution (1024×512)
4. Feed into Canny → ControlNet
5. Initialize EmptyLatentImage at 1024×512
6. Run prompt variations (e.g., "timber cladding," "glass curtain wall," "rammed earth")

Result: Controlled, dimensionally stable façade studies without hallucinated proportions.

## Limitations

- Excessive upscaling (e.g., from 512×512 to 2048×2048) can lead to blurred conditioning or structural breakdown.
- Cropping without re-centering often offsets ControlNet alignment.
- Latent scaling is approximate; for architectural plans or diagrams, prefer pixel-based resizing before encoding.

Resizing and alignment are not trivial pre-processing steps—they are structural guarantees that stabilize generative logic. In architectural workflows, respecting proportion, resolution, and aspect ratio ensures that generative imagery remains interpretable, reusable, and aligned with downstream design goals.

# Chapter 21

# From Sketch to 3D

## Constructing Volumetric Architecture in ComfyUI

Traditionally, architectural workflows progressed from sketch to CAD to 3D modeling and rendering. In the AI age, this sequence can be inverted, compressed, or entirely reimagined. With ComfyUI's evolving capabilities—particularly in 3D voxel inference, latent geometry prediction, and background-aware segmentation—architects can now explore early 3D massing and surface articulation directly from sketches, images, or AI-generated concepts.

This chapter introduces a complete pipeline from 2D sketch or concept image to 3D mesh output, using Hunyuan3D, CLIP vision, REMbg for background removal, and voxel decoding for mesh export. It culminates in .glb or .obj files ready for further refinement in Rhino, Blender, or Unity.

### The Sketch as Latent Architecture

Sketches—whether hand-drawn, diagrammatic, or AI-generated—carry implicit spatial cues. But in diffusion-based systems, these cues must be encoded into latent space representations to become computable. By using CLIP vision encoders and image-to-voxel transformers like Hunyuan3D-diff, we can extract volumetric approximations directly from these images (Fig. 46).

ComfyUI now includes templates for this workflow via:

- Image Only Checkpoint Loader (e.g., hunyuan3d-diff-v2)
- CLIP Vision Encode → for semantic embedding of the sketch
- Hunyuan3DConditioning → to convert embeddings into latent 3D form
- VAEDecodeHunyuan3D → decodes latent into voxel chunks

DOI: 10.1201/9781003637691-23

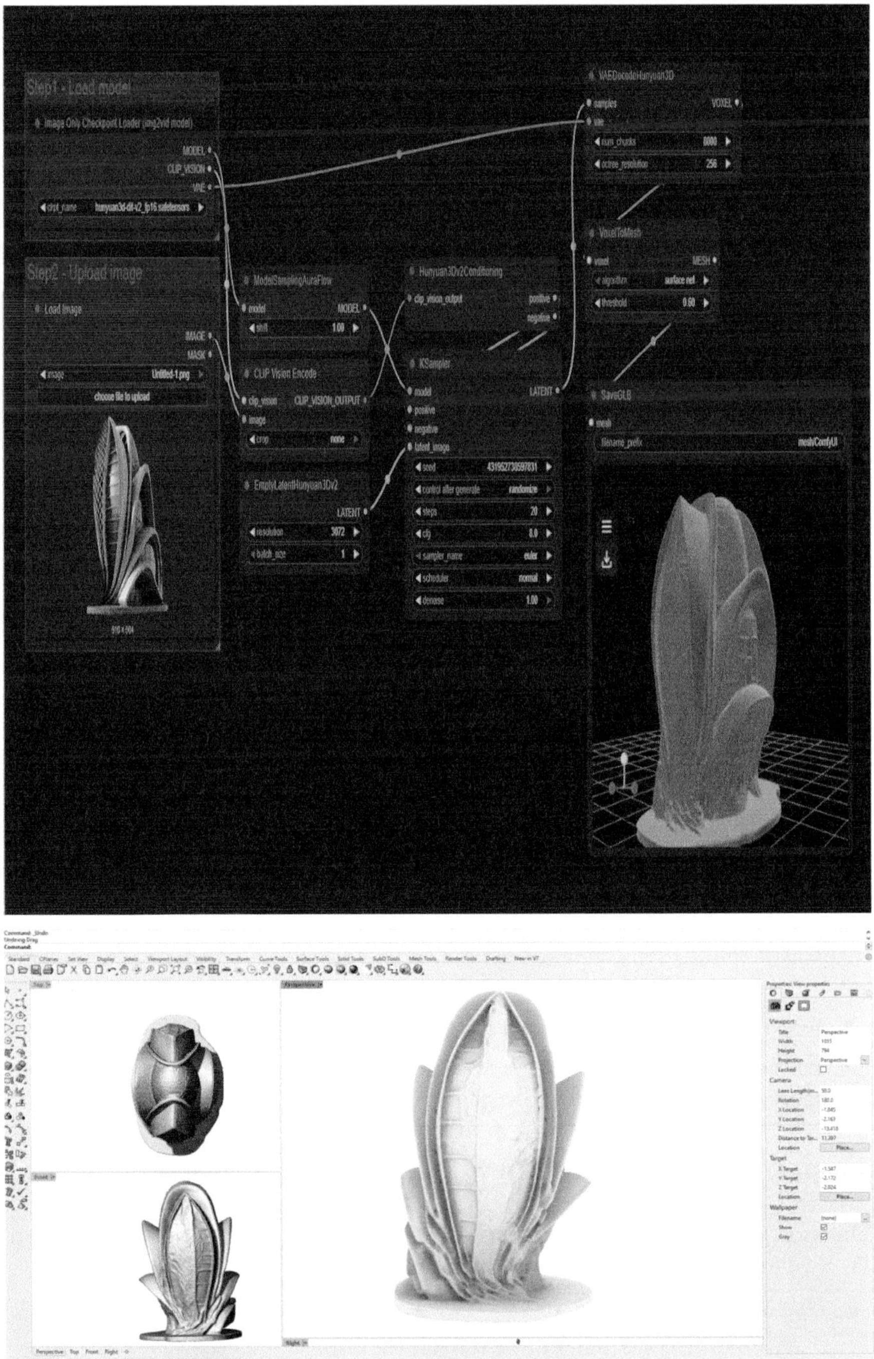


**Figure 46.** Sketch to 3d mesh workflow then imported to Rhino for further enhancement.

- VoxelToMesh → reconstructs a surface mesh
- SaveGLB or SaveOBJ → exports usable 3D file

## Workflow: Sketch to Mesh

### Step 1: Prepare Your Sketch

Your image can be a photo of a hand sketch, a line drawing, or an AI-generated form study. Before processing:

- Ensure good contrast between subject and background.
- Crop to region of interest.
- Save as .png or .jpg.

### Step 2: Remove Background (Optional but Recommended)

To isolate form from visual noise, use the REMbg pipeline:

- Load Image → sketch or concept
- Rembg (Remove Background) node (from ComfyUI-Manager Add-ons)
- Optionally feed this into CLIP Vision Encode

This ensures the 3D model doesn't interpret background elements (e.g., grid paper, shadows) as part of the massing.

### Step 3: Load and Configure Model

Use the node:

Image Only Checkpoint Loader (hunyuan3d-diff-v2_fp16.safetensors)

This checkpoint is trained specifically for *image-to-voxel* inference. Connect:

- CLIP Vision Encode → Hunyuan3DConditioning → KSampler
- Then: KSampler output to VAEDecodeHunyuan3D

Set:

- steps = 20
- cfg = 8.0
- seed = fixed if reproducibility is required

## Mesh Reconstruction and Export

The output of the Hunyuan decoder is a voxel field, not yet a mesh. To convert it:

1. Use VoxelToMesh
   - Algorithm: surface net or marching cubes
   - Threshold: 0.5–0.6 (controls surface density)

2. Use SaveGLB or SaveOBJ
   - You will get a true 3D model for Rhino, Blender, Unity, etc.
   - Example output: an .glb file showing curved, biomorphic architecture from the sketch

## Optional Enhancements: Style, Detail, and Cleanup

Once you generate your base mesh, you may wish to:

- **Refine surfaces** in Blender using Remesh or Subdivision modifiers
- **Boolean merge or slice** with architectural primitives (in Rhino or Grasshopper)
- **UV unwrap and texture** using original sketch elements or AI-generated textures from ComfyUI

You can even return to ComfyUI to retexture your mesh:

- Render views from the 3D model
- Re-enter them into image-to-image pipelines with ControlNet
- Stylize or shade based on daylight, materials, etc.

## Use Cases in Architectural Design

- **Concept Massing**: From AI or hand sketch to printable 3D form
- **Rapid Volumetric Study**: Translate concept visuals into VR-ready formats
- **Site Model Composition**: Generate multiple typologies and integrate into urban models
- **Design Feedback**: Export 3D to collaborators for annotation, testing, or critique

## Technical Limitations and Notes

- This method does not produce accurate scale. Meshes are proportional but not metrically correct.
- Surface quality is non-parametric—useful for study models but not construction-ready.
- Mesh density is tunable but limited by voxel resolution (num_chunks in VAEDecode).
- Architecture with internal voids or complex overhangs may not reconstruct cleanly; it's better suited to expressive or topological massing.

Chapter 22

# Reference-Based Iteration

## Controlling Consistency with IPAdapter, ReferenceOnly, and Latent Anchors

As architectural workflows in ComfyUI evolve from one-shot image generation toward iterative visualization pipelines, maintaining consistency across outputs becomes essential. Whether for multi-view renders, time-based animations, or variant studies, architects increasingly require tools that preserve style, material logic, and spatial identity across frames and viewpoints (Fig. 47).

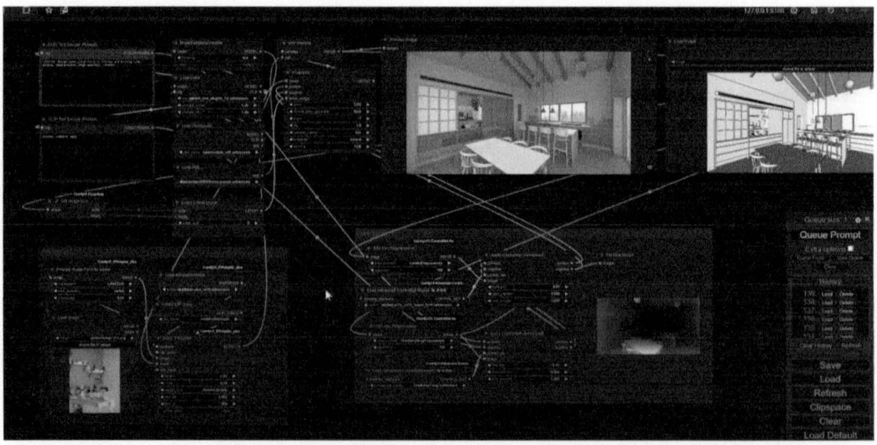


**Figure 47.** IPAdapter workflow (PixelEasel 2024).

DOI: 10.1201/9781003637691-24

## What Is IPAdapter?

IPAdapter (Image Prompt Adapter) is a visual conditioning module developed to transfer high-level style and visual features from a reference image into a diffusion-based generation process. Unlike ControlNet (which controls structure), IPAdapter controls style-space features such as:

- Color palette and lighting tone
- Textural behavior and material logic
- Massing coherence and compositional proportion
- Architectural "language" (formal typologies and detail resolution)

IPAdapter does not require sketch preprocessing or depth maps. Instead, it uses a CLIP Vision encoder to extract semantic features and inject them directly into the denoising stream.

**Recent Variants:**

- IPAdapterXL: Compatible with SDXL and ComfyUI pipelines
- IPAdapterXL Plus: Allows fine-grained regional and layer-wise control
- IPAdapter FaceID: For portrait or human-inhabited architecture shots For architectural tasks, IPAdapterXL is most commonly used.

## IPAdapter Workflow in ComfyUI

**Nodes Required:**

1. LoadImage: Input the reference image
2. IPAdapterModelLoader: Loads the adapter weights (must match the model—SD1.5 or SDXL)
3. IPAdapterEncodeImage: Extracts visual feature embeddings
4. IPAdapterApply: Injects features into the generation stream
5. CLIPTextEncode: Carries the current generation prompt
6. KSampler or KSamplerAdvanced: Performs image generation
7. VAE Decode → SaveImage

Example Architectural Application:

- **Reference Image**: "A brick civic center with translucent roof"
- **Prompt**: "Interior event hall with tiered seating and exposed brick walls"
- **Result**: Style, palette, and texture logic from exterior image are carried into the interior scene.

*You do not need to mention the exact material or form again in the prompt. The IPAdapter will enforce it unless overridden by strong CFG values.*

## ReferenceOnly Node

The ReferenceOnly node is a lightweight alternative to IPAdapter, functioning as a passive latent stylistic hint rather than an injected feature tensor. It is useful for:

- Quick output similarity
- Cross-image atmosphere alignment
- Iteration from previous generations

**Key differences from IPAdapter:**

| Feature | IPAdapter | ReferenceOnly |
|---|---|---|
| Requires trained weights | Yes | No |
| Controls regional style | (in XL Plus) | |
| Fidelity and coherence | Higher | Lower |
| Use Case | Multi-view consistency | Simple reuse and variation |

Use ReferenceOnly when GPU memory is limited or when global style alignment is sufficient.

## Achieving Latent Consistency

Reference-based workflows become even more powerful when combined with latent control techniques, such as:

- **Fixed Seeds**: Guarantees positional and textural consistency
- **Saved Latent Tensors**: Use SaveLatents and LoadLatents nodes to directly re-inject prior generations into new pipelines
- **Latent Noise Injections**: Add minimal controlled variation while preserving overall logic

**Together, these enable:**

- Multi-view perspective generation
- Day/night transitions on the same form
- Design phasing or sequencing without retraining

*Combine fixed seed with IPAdapter for iterative detailing across the same massing structure.*

## Cross-View and Programmatic Variation

With IPAdapter pipelines, you can perform controlled architectural tasks:

- **Exterior → Interior**: Transfer material and envelope logic from the outside to internal spaces
- **Plan → Section → Axo**: Maintain geometry language across orthographic and perspective views
- **Elevation Variants**: Test lighting or façade articulation scenarios using the same core style
- **Functional Prompting**: Change the function (e.g., library, school, mosque) while maintaining materiality and tectonic order

**Example Prompt Progression**:

Reference: Modern timber mosque with high skylight dome

Prompt 1: "Interior prayer hall at dusk, minimal furnishings"

Prompt 2: "Sectional cut showing mezzanine and stairway"

Prompt 3: "Roof-level view showing structural system"

Each retains fidelity to the reference image while exploring design variation.

## Best Practices for Architectural Use

- **Match Aspect Ratio**: Your reference and target image should share dimensions or be proportionally close.
- **Balance CFG and Adapter Strength**: If the text and image compete, reduce CFG (to 5–6) or strengthen image weight.
- **Filter Visual Noise**: Avoid busy or over-decorated reference images.
- **Neutralize Overdominance**: Add modifiers like "monochrome," "ambient lighting," or "no signage" to suppress excess detail.
- **Use Architectural Typologies**: Reinforce discipline using clear typological descriptors (e.g., "low-rise", "atrium-based", "arcaded façade").

## Limitations

- IPAdapter cannot enforce geometric logic; it works best in tandem with ControlNet if structure must remain fixed.
- Style consistency may drift after 2–3 generations if prompt diverges significantly.

- IPAdapterXL is GPU-intensive; optimize batch sizes and resolution.
- SD1.5 and SDXL adapter models are NOT interchangeable—always match model type with adapter variant.

Reference-based conditioning transforms ComfyUI into a multi-stage visualization platform capable of architectural storytelling, design iteration, and diagrammatic simulation. When paired with prompt modulation, ControlNet, and seed anchoring, IPAdapter enables the production of narratively coherent, materially consistent, and spatially diverse outputs—all derived from a unified conceptual seed.

# Chapter 23

# Regional Prompting and Multimodal Control

## Layered Guidance in Architectural Generation

As AI image synthesis moves beyond monolithic prompts and single-control workflows, architects now have access to regionally specific, multimodal control techniques. This chapter introduces methods such as regional prompting with color masks, FluxRegionAttention, and hybrid conditioning using depth, line, style, and mask data in parallel. Together, they offer a precision toolkit for spatial logic, façade articulation, and program differentiation within a single render.

These techniques are especially valuable in architectural workflows that require heterogeneous materiality, functional zoning, or multi-style representation in the same composition—for example, a building with brick base, glass midsection, and green rooftop.

### What is Regional Prompting?

Regional prompting refers to the ability to guide different parts of an image using localized text descriptions, each assigned to a spatial region (usually color-coded masks). Rather than one global prompt, the model interprets regions according to their assigned semantic content (Fig. 48).

This approach is enabled by models trained with or adapted to regional attention maps. Two dominant workflows support this:

- **Color Mask Prompting** (e.g., with *Regional Prompting in AnimateDiff or IPAdapter Regional*)

DOI: 10.1201/9781003637691-25

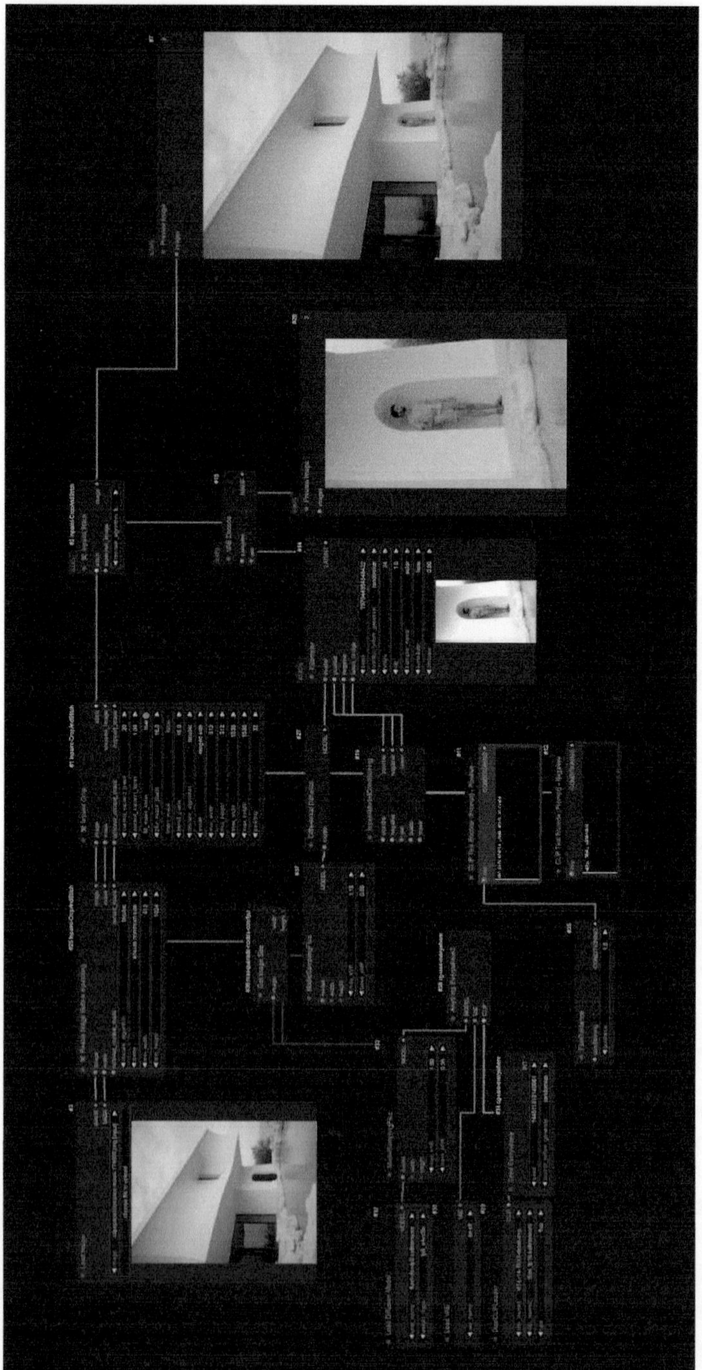

**Figure 48.** Inpainting workflow (Cybertect 2024).

- **FluxRegionAttention**, developed by the Flux team, enabling region-wise prompt injection in SDXL pipelines.

## ComfyUI Workflows for Regional Control

### a. Color-Mask Based Regional Prompting

This method involves using an input segmentation or color-coded mask where each color is mapped to a different prompt. For example:

- **Red** = "concrete façade with deep-set windows"
- **Blue** = "glazed curtain wall with aluminum frame"
- **Green** = "vegetated rooftop with timber pergola"

**Workflow:**

1. Node: LoadImage (Color Mask PNG)
2. Node: ColorPromptSelector
3. Node: RegionalPromptEncoder
4. Node: RegionalControlUNet
5. Combine with global prompt or latent initialization
6. Sampler (KSampler / AnimateDiff)

**Output**: Each region is interpreted and rendered according to its designated style.

### b. FluxRegionAttention in ComfyUI

The FluxRegionAttention extension adds regional control to SDXL pipelines. It parses a UV coordinate map or color mask and injects localized attention during the denoising process. The user assigns text prompts to specific regions defined by color.

**Workflow:**

1. Node: FluxRegionLoader
2. Node: FluxMaskDecoder (interprets color-region)
3. Node: PromptToRegionMap
4. Connect to modified KSampler compatible with Flux pipeline

## Combining Depth + Lineart + Style + Mask

While ComfyUI allows multiple ControlNets in parallel, a more nuanced approach is to condition the image via *orthogonal modalities*. This gives both structural and stylistic constraints without overriding the model's creative plasticity.

**Multi-modal conditioning workflow:**

- ControlNet 1: Lineart — for structural edges and form logic
- ControlNet 2: Depth map — for lighting and volumetric massing
- ControlNet 3: Style reference — for texture and material tone
- ControlNet 4: Masked regions — for zonal prompt targeting

Each ControlNet is given a moderate Control Weight (0.8–1.2) and distinct Start/End Percent values, enabling temporal layering during denoising.

## Best Practices for Architectural Prompts with Region Control

- Match resolution of mask to your EmptyLatentImage node.
- Always verify that color regions do not overlap or alias—use clear boundaries.
- Avoid too many regions (3–5 recommended) to preserve output stability.
- Use simple, distinct materials per region ("wood," "glass," "green roof") to reduce hallucination.
- Use reference image styles globally if coherence across zones is desired.

## Limitations and Considerations

- These workflows are not natively supported in every model; they require SDXL-compatible regional models or patched samplers (e.g., AnimateDiff Regional, Flux UNet).
- Color masks must be clean, high-resolution, and RGB-coded. Avoid grayscale or fuzzy masks.
- Some combinations (e.g., depth + region prompts) may lead to instability if improperly weighted.
- Not ideal for ultra-photorealistic renders yet—currently best for design exploration, conceptual visualizations, and style mapping.

## Suggested Applications in Practice

- Façade Design Toolkits: Combine sketch-based elevation with regional material assignment.

- Zoning Studies: Use masks to simulate massing differentiation across program types.
- Studio Pedagogy: Teach students material articulation and typological contrasts in a single output.
- Narrative Sections: Color-coded sections prompt different interior programs, lighting styles, or time-of-day moods.

Chapter 24

# Integrating AI into Grasshopper with APIs, MCP, and Assistant Plugins

## Understanding APIs

An API (Application Programming Interface) is essentially a set of rules and endpoints that allow different software systems to communicate and exchange data. In practical terms, an API is like a bridge between applications – one application (the client) sends a request (for some data or service) to another application or service (the server), and the server sends back a response through the API. This communication is typically done over the internet using web APIs (often via HTTP requests). APIs enable developers (and end-users indirectly) to leverage external services' functionality without having to build those capabilities from scratch.

For architects and designers working with tools like Rhino and Grasshopper, APIs open the door to integrating powerful external services—for example, generative AI models/ LLMs–directly into design workflows. Instead of treating an AI like ChatGPT or Claude as a separate tool, you can use their API to connect them with Grasshopper. This means Grasshopper (via a script or plugin) can send a prompt or data to an AI service and get back a result (text, numbers, or even code) within your design environment. By using APIs, architects can automate or augment certain tasks: imagine Grasshopper asking an AI to generate a pattern algorithm, to suggest code for a complex geometry, or even to control Rhino with natural-language commands—all possible through the API connection. In summary, the API is the mechanism that allows Grasshopper to talk to AI models. The architect provides a prompt or request (like "Generate a parametric facade pattern with adjustable wave amplitude") and the AI service returns a response (perhaps code

DOI: 10.1201/9781003637691-26

or instructions to create that pattern). The API handles authentication (using an API key), formatting the request, and returning the AI's answer in a structured way. This general framework underpins many of the new AI-driven tools we'll discuss.

## Connecting Grasshopper to AI Models via API

How can we actually hook up Grasshopper to an AI like OpenAI's ChatGPT, Anthropic's Claude, or Google's Gemini? There are a few approaches, ranging from custom scripting to specialized protocols and plugins. Below we outline the main methods along with their workflows:

- **Direct API Calls with Scripting:** One straightforward way is to use Grasshopper's scripting components (C# or Python) to call an AI service's API directly. In this workflow, you would:
  1. **Obtain API Credentials** – e.g., get an API key from OpenAI, Claude, etc., which authorizes your requests.
  2. **Formulate a Request** – craft a prompt or query in your Grasshopper script. This could be a question or an instruction for the AI (for instance, asking for code or a design solution).
  3. **Make the HTTP Request** – Use a library or built-in web functionality to send the prompt to the AI's REST API endpoint. For example, with Python you might use the requests library to POST to OpenAI's API endpoint with your prompt and key.
  4. **Receive and Parse the Response** – The AI will return a response (often in JSON). Your script then reads this response. If the result is just text (say a description or a number), you can use it directly. If it's code (e.g., Python script text or JSON describing a Grasshopper definition), you might need to pass it into another component or execute it.
  5. **Apply in Grasshopper** – Finally, use the AI's output in your GH definition. For instance, if the AI returned some geometry parameters, you plug them into creating geometry; if it returned code, you could execute it to create components or perform an action.

Example: Suppose you want ChatGPT to help design a parametric pattern. You could write a GH Python component that sends a prompt like "Give me Python code that creates 10 sliders and uses their values to move points in a sine wave pattern". The API returns a block of code or instructions. Your script can then create those sliders via the Grasshopper API or output the code for you to review. In practice, some have tried similar things – with varying success – by manually asking ChatGPT for

Grasshopper scripts and copying them into GH. Early experiments in 2023 showed that ChatGPT didn't always fully understand Grasshopper's API, sometimes producing incorrect code (e.g., trying to use Rhino document objects instead of Grasshopper classes). Newer models (GPT-4 and beyond) are improving at these niche tasks, but the principle remains: you can leverage the API directly, just be prepared to debug the AI's output.

- **Using the Model Context Protocol (MCP):** A more structured approach to connecting AI with design tools is through emerging standards like Claude's *Model Context Protocol (MCP)*. MCP is an open-source protocol that enables secure, two-way connections between AI agents and external applications. In simpler terms, MCP defines a standard way for an AI to send commands to and receive data from software like Rhino/Grasshopper.

One example is the Grasshopper MCP Bridge, an open-source project that connects Grasshopper with Claude's AI via MCP. The Grasshopper MCP Bridge sets up a local server and a GH plugin that together act as a middleman between Claude and Grasshopper. Some key features of this system include:

- **High-Level Commands:** You can give Claude a natural language instruction (even complex ones), and via MCP the system will create or modify Grasshopper components to fulfill the request. For instance, you might say *"Create a series of circles along a sine curve and loft them"* – the AI, with MCP, can translate that into actual GH component operations (MCP Grasshopper).
- **Component Knowledge Base:** The bridge provides Claude with a knowledge base of Grasshopper components, their parameters, and how they connect. This helps the AI make valid solutions (it knows what each component does and how to wire them correctly).
- **Two-Way Control:** MCP allows the AI not just to send commands but also to *read* context. For example, Claude could query the existing state of the GH canvas or Rhino model through the protocol, making the interaction stateful. This two-way link is more advanced than a one-off API call, enabling a kind of back-and-forth *"agent"* behavior.

The workflow for MCP integration is a bit involved but instructive:

1. You install a Grasshopper plugin (GH_MCP.gha) which opens a local TCP server inside Rhino/Grasshopper.
2. You run a Python-based bridge server that connects to Claude (either Claude Cloud or Claude Desktop) and listens to the GH server.

3. When you send a prompt to Claude (through a chat interface), Claude's responses in MCP format are routed to the Grasshopper plugin, which then executes the specified operations (creating components, adjusting sliders, baking geometry, etc.). These are transferred through JSON fiels, that contain component information, patterns, and intenets.

Using MCP, architects and designers can control Rhino/Grasshopper with natural language. The MCP approach is powerful, though currently more of an experimental toolkit; it showcases what future AI-driven design assistants might look like under the hood.

- **Leveraging Existing Plugins and APIs:** Before rolling your own scripts from scratch, note that many new Grasshopper plugins already handle a lot of this API communication for you. (We'll discuss specific plugins in the next section.) These tools abstract the API calls into a friendly UI – you might just type or speak a prompt inside Grasshopper, and behind the scenes the plugin calls the AI API, then translates the answer into GH actions. For example:
    - **GHPT (Grasshopper + GPT)** was an early prototype from 2023 that let users enter a text prompt to generate a Grasshopper definition. The plugin would send the prompt to ChatGPT and receive a structured JSON describing what components to place and how to connect them. It then instantiated those components on the canvas automatically. This hackathon project illustrated the potential: ChatGPT was effectively "coding" a GH script from your description.
    - **Voice Inputs:** Some integrations even allow voice as input. Since voice can be converted to text (using speech-to-text APIs) and then fed to the AI, you can literally talk to Grasshopper. For instance, the WOLF plugin (described below) demonstrated "voice-to-Grasshopper" functionality – an architect could speak a design intent and the system would create the corresponding parametric setup. This works by simply layering a speech recognition API in front of the AI API, making the workflow hands-free.

In short, connecting Grasshopper to AI through APIs can be done at different levels of complexity. Beginners might start by manually asking ChatGPT for help with scripting (copy-pasting code), while advanced users or developers can set up direct API scripts or even an MCP server for real-time control. Regardless of method, the ability to bring AI into your parametric design process offers huge possibilities – from automating routine tasks to exploring creative solutions that you generate by "chatting" with your tools.

## AI Assistant Plugins for Grasshopper (Wolf, Raven, & More)

Over the last couple of years, several AI-driven assistant plugins for Grasshopper have emerged. These plugins act as co-pilots for parametric design, allowing you to use natural language (and sometimes images) to create or modify Grasshopper definitions. We'll cover some of the leading tools – Wolf, Raven, SmartHopper, Kea, and others – and how they differ. All of these rely on APIs under the hood (often OpenAI or similar), but they package the AI in a way that's convenient for architects and designers.

### WOLF – Natural Language to Grasshopper

WOLF is a free AI-powered Grasshopper plugin introduced in 2025, and it fundamentally changes how you can create definitions. With WOLF, you simply describe what you want to build in plain English, and it generates a complete Grasshopper script for you – components, wires, and all. It's essentially a chatbot inside Grasshopper: you "chat" with WOLF about your design intent, and it translates that into parametric logic.

Key features of WOLF include:

- Chat Interface: You can type requests or questions in natural language (and reportedly even use voice input in demonstrations) to communicate with WOLF. For example: "Create a series of points in a spiral and connect them with a curve".
- Instant GH Script Generation: WOLF instantly places Grasshopper components on the canvas according to your description, connecting them appropriately. If you said "spiral points", it might drop a range component, a polar array or spiral logic, construct points, etc., all wired up.
- Precision Control: It offers advanced AI search settings where you can adjust how closely it matches your request. This likely means you can dial the creativity or randomness up/down – either get very literal results or allow more interpretive results.
- Iterative Design: Although WOLF's initial version is geared towards one-off generation, you can presumably refine by telling WOLF to adjust something ("now make the spiral radius larger" or "add a slider for the height") and it would modify the canvas accordingly.

### Raven – Full-Featured AI Design Partner

Raven is another influential Grasshopper AI assistant, developed by the startup Romantic Technology. It launched earlier (around late 2024) and has matured into a robust, cross-platform tool. While WOLF focuses on generating scripts from scratch, Raven goes further: it can generate, edit,

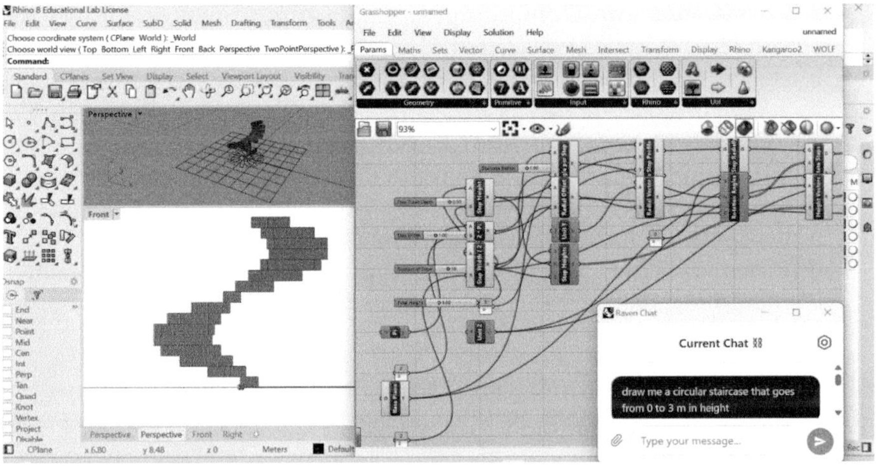


**Figure 49.** Raven Chatbot.

and even iteratively refine Grasshopper scripts via a chat interface, using generative AI.

In practice, architects using Raven have found they can very quickly prototype complex definitions by simply describing the goal. For example, "Generate a hexagonal grid facade with random openings" could yield a full parametric setup in seconds. Then you might say, "Now make the openings respond to an attractor point", and Raven would alter the definition accordingly by adding the needed nodes (like a distance-based scaling). This ability to iterate conversationally is Raven's standout advantage.

### SmartHopper – Open-Source AI Assistant (Context-Aware)

SmartHopper is another AI assistant plugin, notable for being open-source (under LGPL license) and for how it interprets existing Grasshopper definitions. Developed by Marc Roca (announced mid-2025), SmartHopper aims to help users learn Grasshopper and solve problems by embedding AI guidance directly in the tool.

Key aspects of SmartHopper:

- **Reads Your GH Canvas:** SmartHopper can convert your entire Grasshopper definition into a JSON representation (using the GhJSON format) and send that to an AI model. This means the AI "sees" what components you've placed, how they're connected, what values are present, etc. Because of this, the AI's responses can be highly specific – it could debug an error in your definition, suggest which component is misconfigured, or give tips on how to achieve something within *your* exact script.

- **AI Assistance for Debugging and Learning:** Since it knows the structure of your canvas, SmartHopper can do things like point out mistakes, recommend fixes or optimizations, or even explain what a cluster of components is doing (great for learning). For example, if your definition isn't working, you could ask, "Why am I getting empty geometry here?" The AI (with the canvas data) might respond, "The 'Curve Divide' component has zero length curves input, causing null points – consider filtering those out." This is a fundamentally different use-case from just generating a whole script from scratch; it's about augmenting the user's understanding and troubleshooting capabilities.

### DIY: Using Python to Query AI (Manual Workflow)

While plugins like Raven and Kea provide ready-made interfaces, you might wonder how to do a basic manual integration yourself. This could be for learning purposes, or perhaps to customize the AI interaction in a way no plugin currently supports. We touched on direct API calls earlier; here we'll outline a simple example of using Grasshopper's Python scripting component to ask an AI for something and use the result.

Scenario: You want to use ChatGPT to generate some geometry in Grasshopper – for example, create a series of points following a mathematical pattern – and you want it to include sliders so you can tweak the pattern. Essentially, you're asking GPT to be your coder.

Step-by-step manual approach:

1. **Get your API setup:** Suppose you have an OpenAI API key (for ChatGPT). You'll need to have that ready. Also ensure your system can make HTTP requests. (In GH's standard IronPython, you might use the System.Net libraries or the urllib module since installing external packages like requests could be tricky. Alternatively, use a CPython integration or GhPython remote if needed.)
2. **Formulate the prompt clearly:** In a GH Python component, you write a string prompt to send. For example:
3. **prompt** = "Write Grasshopper C# script code that adds 5 Number Slider components on the canvas and connects each to a Point component to create a wave pattern of points. The sliders should control amplitude, frequency, phase, etc."

This prompt explicitly asks for code (in C# in this case, because adding actual GH objects via script might be easier with GH API calls in C#). You could also ask for Python code that uses RhinoCommon/Grasshopper, but ensure the AI knows the context (ChatGPT might not know GH API methods offhand unless told).

4. **Make the API call in Python:** Using a library or .NET method, you send this prompt to the OpenAI API endpoint. For example, via HTTP POST to https://api.openai.com/v1/chat/completions with the appropriate headers (Authorization with your key) and body (model = gpt-4, prompt = above, etc.). The GH Python component can execute this call and wait for the response. This is essentially replicating what the plugins do internally.
5. **Receive the response:** The API will return a JSON with the AI's answer. You parse the JSON to extract the message content, which should be the code (and possibly some explanation text).
6. **Use the code in Grasshopper:** Now you have (in this hypothetical scenario) a piece of C# code as a string. What next? You could do a couple of things:
   - Easiest: Print it or output it from the Python component, so you (the human) can create a C# Script component in GH, paste the code and run it. The code, if correct, would then add sliders and points to the canvas (Fig. 50).
   - Advanced: You could actually execute the code directly via the Grasshopper API. For example, the Python script could use Grasshopper.Kernel.GH_Document methods to add sliders programmatically (which is what the C# code would do anyway). In effect, you might not need the intermediate code if you can have the AI return a structured plan. But that requires more coding on your part to interpret instructions.
   - Alternatively, ask the AI to return a JSON of component placements (like GHPT did). Then your script can iterate that JSON and create the components via Grasshopper SDK calls. This is quite involved, so typically one would rely on plugins like GHPT/Wolf that already handle it.
7. **Maintain conversation (optional):** If you want to refine the result, you might call the API again with a follow-up prompt, including the conversation history. For example, "Now make those sliders range from 0 to 100 and label them appropriately." Maintaining context means you have to send the previous messages along with the new request (OpenAI's API allows sending a list of messages to simulate a conversation). In a quick one-off script, you'd handle this manually by concatenating or storing the history between runs. This is where doing it yourself becomes cumbersome – which is exactly why tools like Raven and Kea, that handle conversation state, are so valuable.

Doing this manually requires some programming ability and understanding of how to call web services. Additionally, as users found, ChatGPT might not always get Grasshopper-specific code right on the first try. You may need to iterate, or even manually correct the AI's suggestions. There's also the fact that running external calls from within Grasshopper can introduce delays (each API call might take a couple of seconds or more, during which Grasshopper is waiting).

However, this exercise is educational – it shows the mechanics behind the scenes. Essentially, any AI Grasshopper plugin is doing exactly these steps: taking your prompt, calling an API, and then doing something with the answer (placing components, writing script code, etc.). By attempting it yourself, you get fine-grained control. For instance, you could integrate a very specific AI model (maybe a custom-trained one) or impose additional logic on the AI's output before using it.

In practice, many architects might use a hybrid approach: use ChatGPT (or another AI) in a separate window to discuss a problem and get code scripts, then manually bring those into Rhino/Grasshopper Python.

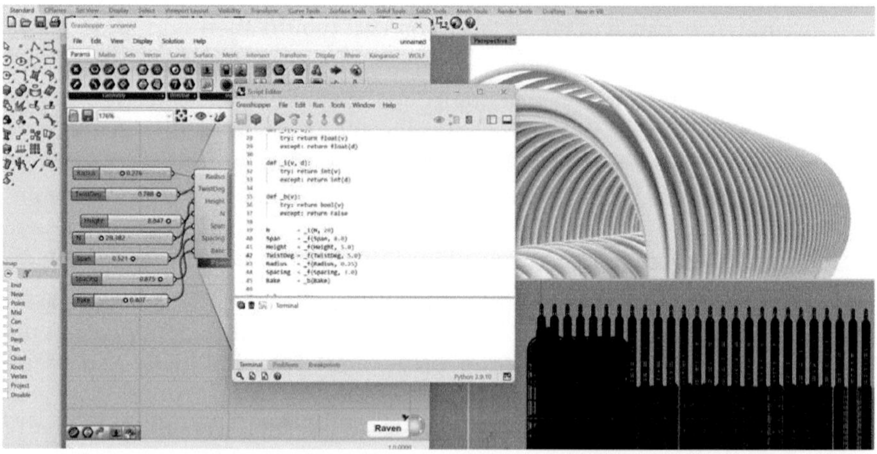

**Figure 50.** Manual connection between Python, Grasshopper, and ChatGPT.

## Beyond Grasshopper: Dynamo and BIM with AI (Gemini, etc.)

While Rhino and Grasshopper are at the forefront of AI-assisted design workflows, similar developments are happening in the BIM world, particularly with Autodesk Revit and Dynamo. Dynamo is to Revit what Grasshopper is to Rhino – a visual programming tool for parametric BIM. Architects and BIM specialists are beginning to hook up AI models to Dynamo for generative and analytical tasks.

These cutting-edge examples highlight that AI integration is not limited to Grasshopper. The concept of an "AI assistant" can apply to any design software with programmatic access. Revit's API combined with Dynamo scripts can achieve similar results – whether it's creating geometry from prompts (Text-to-BIM) or providing reasoning on design decisions (AI critique and guidance).

**BIM-specific AI assistants**: While not as public yet as the Grasshopper plugins, we can imagine tools emerging for Revit/Dynamo similar to Raven or SmartHopper. For example, a Dynamo AI that you chat with to create automation scripts, or a Revit "CoPilot" that can respond to commands like "Check this model for code compliance issues" or "Generate layout options for this floor plan". Some startups and research projects (like Autodesk's research or Hypar with AI) are exploring these directions.

# Chapter 25

# Integrating ComfyUI with Grasshopper

## Parametric Data to Prompt-Driven Visualization

Parametric modeling and latent image synthesis represent a new dialectic in architectural design. While Grasshopper, the visual programming environment for Rhino3D, formalizes geometric intelligence and rule-based systems, ComfyUI translates abstract prompts and visual guidance into evocative, atmospheric, and stylistic imagery. The true power lies not in choosing one over the other, but in their sophisticated synthesis.

This chapter details methods for bridging these two systems. This is not a guide for simple image export, but a technical blueprint for creating a dynamic, synchronous feedback loop. We will move beyond manual file transfers and establish a seamless connection, leveraging data and control maps to augment parametric possibility with prompt-driven narrative.

## The Case for a Technical Bridge: Augmentation over Substitution

The integration of Grasshopper and ComfyUI is not about replacing one process with another. It's about creating a complementary, non-destructive workflow:

- **From Geometry to Atmosphere:** Translate algorithmically-driven forms into compelling, high-fidelity renders with a single slider change.

DOI: 10.1201/9781003637691-27

- **From Performance to Narrative:** Visualize environmental or structural analysis data not as a sterile heatmap, but as a richly textured, architecturally-coherent scene.
- **From Rules to Affect:** Embed logical design constraints directly into a stylistic scene, ensuring the AI output respects the underlying tectonic or formal intention.

The goal is to create a responsive, iterative design environment where parametric manipulation immediately translates to stylistic speculation, accelerating the ideation process from hours to seconds.

## Strategy 1: The Static Export Workflow

Before we build a live bridge, it is crucial to master the foundational workflow. This method, while manual, provides the highest degree of control and serves as the conceptual basis for automation.

**Pipeline Structure:**

1. **Grasshopper to Visual Map:** Use Grasshopper to generate geometry, then use a Rhino viewport or a dedicated component to capture and save a specific visual representation.
2. **Visual Map to ControlNet:** In ComfyUI, load this visual map as a ControlNet input, using a preprocessor to extract specific features.
3. **ControlNet + Prompt to AI Render:** Combine the ControlNet output with a detailed prompt and a robust sampling pipeline.

**Technical Execution: The Multi-ControlNet Approach**

For maximum fidelity, do not export a single image. Export multiple, precisely aligned feature maps to condition the AI on different aspects of the geometry simultaneously.

- **Rhino/Grasshopper Side:**
  - **Canny Edges:** Use a Make2D command or a Python script to extract linework. Export as a high-contrast, transparent .png.
  - **Depth Map:** Set up a custom material or shader in Rhino that colors geometry based on distance from the camera (Z-buffer). Export this as a grayscale .png. This is critical for volumetric control.
  - **Normal Map (Advanced):** Use a custom render engine or a dedicated plugin to export a normal map, which encodes the surface orientation as an RGB image. This is the single best method for preserving micro-surface detail.

- **ComfyUI Side:**
  - **Load Multiple Controls:** Use three separate ControlNetLoader nodes and connect them to the main KSampler pipeline.
  - **Preprocessors:** For each ControlNet, use the corresponding preprocessor node (e.g., Canny Preprocessor, MiDaS-depth Preprocessor, Normal Preprocessor).
  - **Input Alignment:** Crucially, ensure the resolution of your Grasshopper-exported images (e.g., 1024x768) perfectly matches the EmptyLatentImage node in ComfyUI. Any misalignment will lead to artifacts.

This multi-ControlNet setup gives the AI explicit instructions on not just the outline of the form, but its depth and surface orientation, allowing the prompt to focus purely on stylistic and atmospheric qualities.

## Strategy 2: The ComfyUI API Live Bridge

This is the integration of a dynamic, quasi-synchronous workflow where changing a Grasshopper slider triggers an immediate, updated AI render. This requires leveraging the ComfyUI server's API via scripting.

**The DIY Pipeline:**

1. **Grasshopper as Data Source:** Use Grasshopper components (e.g., Sliders, Number, Text) to generate parametric data (window_count, facade_material).
2. **Python Scripting:** In Grasshopper, use a Python Script component to assemble this data into a structured JSON payload.
3. **API Request:** The Python script sends this JSON payload via a POST request to the ComfyUI server's /prompt endpoint.
4. **ComfyUI as Render Engine:** The ComfyUI server receives the request, queues the render, and outputs the final image to a watch folder.

A Step-by-Step Technical Blueprint:

- **Step 1: ComfyUI Server Setup:**
  - Start ComfyUI with the --listen flag to enable API access.
  - Create a base ComfyUI workflow that has inputs for a prompt and a ControlNet image. Save this workflow as a .json file.
  - The .json file contains a graph of nodes. We will programmatically inject new prompt text and new image data into this graph.
- **Step 2: Grasshopper Scripting (Python)**:

- Use the requests library in your Python script to make the API call.
- Load your base .json workflow graph into the script.
- Dynamically update specific nodes in the graph. For example:
  - Find the Prompt node and update its text string with data from your Grasshopper sliders.
  - Find the LoadImage node for ControlNet and update its filename to the path of a newly exported image.
- Send the modified graph as a JSON payload to the /prompt endpoint:

## Strategy 3: Real-Time Stream with Screen Share (Mixlab)

While a direct API connection offers programmatic control, a different approach—leveraging screen-sharing—provides a more immediate, visual feedback loop suitable for live design sessions and rapid ideation. The Mixlab Screen Share Mixlab custom node bypasses file I/O and API calls by capturing a designated area of the screen and feeding it directly into a ComfyUI workflow. This is particularly effective for workflows where the visual output from Grasshopper/Rhino is the primary input, not a data-driven text prompt.

**The Live "Visual" Bridge:**

1. **Grasshopper as Live Canvas:** Set up your Grasshopper definition and its corresponding Rhino viewport. Use a combination of custom display settings, Human UI components, or even Anemone loops to create a dynamic, changing visual output in the viewport. This could be a Canny-like line drawing, a depth-shaded render, or a simple massing diagram.
2. **ComfyUI as Observer:** In ComfyUI, install the comfyui-mixlab-nodes custom node set. The Screen Share Mixlab node acts as the entry point of your workflow.
3. **Define the Capture Region:** When you activate the Screen Share node, it will prompt you to select a region of your screen. Carefully draw a box around your Rhino viewport. This is the "live data" source for ComfyUI.
4. **Connect to ControlNet:** Connect the current frame (image) output of the Screen Share node directly to the image input of a ControlNet Preprocessor node (e.g., Canny Preprocessor, MiDaS-depth Preprocessor). This is the critical step: the live stream becomes your control map.

5. **Set Refresh Rate and Prompting:** Set a low refresh_rate (e.g., 250–500 ms) to ensure a fluid connection. Combine the ControlNet output with your desired text prompt and run the workflow in "Live" or "Auto Queue" mode.

**Advantages and Technical Nuances:**

- **Zero File Overhead:** This method completely eliminates the latency and I/O overhead of saving and loading files. The data stream is in memory, making it incredibly fast.
- **Intuitive Feedback:** This is the most "direct" form of interaction. As you manipulate geometry in Grasshopper (e.g., move a point, change a slider), the Rhino viewport updates, and the ComfyUI output updates almost instantly. It creates a powerful, visual, cause-and-effect loop that feels genuinely real-time.
- **Prompt Override Control:** You can use the prompt input parameter in the Screen Share node to dynamically influence the generation, but this is a secondary concern. The power of this workflow lies in the visual, geometric input dominating the AI's composition.

**Limitations and Expert Workarounds:**

- **Single-View Limitation:** The node only captures a single screen region. This prevents the advanced multi-ControlNet workflows (Canny + Depth + Normal) we discussed earlier, as it cannot capture three different feature maps simultaneously.
- **Platform Dependency:** This method may not work reliably across all operating systems or with specific desktop environments. It is highly dependent on the screen-capturing APIs available to the node.
- **No Parametric Prompting:** You cannot programmatically inject parametric data (e.g., from a number slider) directly into a prompt within this workflow. The prompt is a static input within ComfyUI, meaning the connection is purely visual, not data-driven.

While the Mixlab Screen Share node lacks the raw programmatic power of an API call, it excels in its simplicity and immediacy, offering an alternative path to creating a genuinely reactive design environment for live ideation and presentation. It is a perfect tool for a design crit or a real-time exploration session where the visual is paramount and the underlying parametric data is assumed.

```
# URL of your ComfyUI server
comfy_api = "http://127.0.0.1:8188/prompt"
# Load your base workflow
with open("your_workflow.json", "r") as f:
 prompt_json = json.load(f)
# --- Dynamic updates from Grasshopper ---
# Update the prompt text based on a GH input
prompt_json["prompt"]["3"]["inputs"]["text"] = "A brutalist villa with " + str(window_count)
+ " windows"
# Update the ControlNet image path based on GH exported file
prompt_json["prompt"]["11"]["inputs"]["image"] = "C:/path/to/exported_image.png"
# Send the request to ComfyUI
response = requests.post(comfy_api, json=prompt_json)
print(f"ComfyUI Response: {response.text}")
```

- **Step 3: Grasshopper to File:**
  - Crucially, you need a component to save the ControlNet images to a specific folder every time a slider is changed. This is where the Human UI Capture Viewport or a dedicated Python script comes in. The Python script from Step 2 will reference this newly saved file.

This pipeline creates a powerful, non-blocking asynchronous loop that translates parametric changes into AI-driven visualizations in real-time.

## From Data to Prompt: The "Parametric Prompt"

Moving beyond a simple API trigger, we can use Grasshopper to generate the prompt itself. This is where the true power of data-driven design merges with AI.

**Methodology:**

1. **Define Parametric Variables:** In Grasshopper, define key design parameters:
   - FacadeMaterial_String (e.g., "CLT panels," "corrugated metal")
   - StructuralLogic_String (e.g., "post-and-beam," "waffle slab")

   - LightingCondition_String (e.g., "golden hour," "overcast morning")
   - FormLanguage_String (e.g., "brutalist," "organic")
2. **Concatenate into a Prompt:** Use a Text component in Grasshopper to combine these variables into a single, cohesive prompt string.
3. **Inject into ComfyUI:** Send this complete prompt string into a ComfyUI workflow JSON (e.g., as input to a CLIPTextEncode node). This can be done via the ComfyUI API or WebSocket interface.

**Example:** Grasshopper Text Component: "A " + FormLanguage_String + " villa with " + FacadeMaterial_String + " structure. Rendered during a " + LightingCondition_String + "."

This allows you to explore entire design spaces by simply changing a drop-down menu or a slider, generating a series of images that are not just different, but semantically and parametrically distinct.

## 25.6 Limitations and Expert Considerations

- **Non-Evaluative AI Outputs:** ComfyUI does not understand physics. The image may look convincing, but it does not simulate structure, environmental performance, or code. It is an aesthetic tool, not an analytical one.
- **Latency Management:** The time from API call to image generation is a function of GPU load. Implement a queueing system or a delay in your Grasshopper script to prevent overwhelming the ComfyUI server during rapid slider changes.
- **Prompt-Geometry Tension:** A poorly-phrased prompt can override your ControlNet's geometric instructions. For example, a "soft, flowing building" prompt may distort a rigid Canny line drawing. Learn to balance the weight of your prompts and ControlNet inputs.
- **The Bridge is Not a Product:** This is a custom solution. It requires a deep understanding of both environments and is prone to break with version updates. It is a tool for a specialist, not a simple plug-and-play solution.

The Comfy-Hopper Nexus is a profound tool for the modern architect. By creating a custom API bridge, we transform Grasshopper from a purely geometric engine into a narrative command center. The result is a workflow where design intelligence, codified in parameters, is instantly translated into visual poetry. This doesn't replace the architect—it empowers them, turning tedious rendering into an act of real-time, speculative design. This is not just a technical trick; it is a fundamental shift in how we conceive of, explore, and communicate architectural ideas.

# Chapter 26

# KreaAI and Google's Nano Banana

We will work with three tools that complement one another across the arc from idea to editable 3D. KreaAI is our fast ideation surface. It gives immediate visual feedback while you type, draw, or blend references, so you can search for form, light, and material attitude in minutes. Google's Nano Banana is our control stage. It takes a chosen frame and produces consistent variations from it, obeying localized instructions without masks and preserving the identity of the scene across edits. At a final stage you can use any 2d to 3d creator, whether through NVIDIA PartPacker, ComfyUI, MeshyAI, Hunyuan, etc., to create the 3d object out of it read for 3d printing. NVIDIA's new PartPacker works differently than the others, as it is capable of creating the mesh in parts, so you are able to remove, modify, add parts at the convenience of the user, rather than having the whole 3d object as one bulk of mesh.

We use them in this order because each solves a distinct problem, however this is not a rule of moving forward in the same sequence. In the following workflow, the usage took place in that sequence to show an example of how one idea could develop around available platforms.

## KreaAI as a live ideation instrument

KreaAI is a browser platform for generative images and video that distinguishes itself by a Realtime canvas. As you type, nudge sliders, or draw, the image updates instantly. The system accepts text prompts, image references, and even webcam feeds, and it lets you tune model influence during generation, which is decisive when you want to steer rather than surrender the outcome. Krea aggregates several state-of-the-art models behind a unified interface and exposes Realtime, Image, Video,

DOI: 10.1201/9781003637691-28

and Enhancer tools for upscaling and style coherence. The result is a very fast feedback loop suitable for early architectural exploration.

Krea has several other options integrated; image generation, video generation, Realtime editor, motion transfer, creating 3D objects, enhancing, editing, and video restyling. Additionally, Krea has an option where you can train your own LoRA.

Krea's Realtime canvas supports instant updates from text and references, lets you inject external visual feeds, and includes strength controls that modulate how aggressively the AI overrides your input.

## Krea session

Use Krea to grow a candidate image you will later refine in Nano Banana. Treat it like quick charcoal studies before a measured drawing. Nano Banana and Krea are already connected on the platform as well.

- Open Krea Realtime.
- Pick a base style or start from a blank canvas.
- Add your image, or generate one through the connected Nano Banana platform
- Paste a compact architectural prompt, for example: "Futuristic architecture."
- Click Add Reference and drop a precedent facade or a massing sketch to anchor geometry and material vocabulary.
- Set Influence to a moderate value so the model bends toward your reference rather than ignoring it.
- Paint broad silhouettes on the canvas to block massing.
- Play around with the bulk of tools available, and finally export the most promising frame at the highest available resolution and save the prompt state for provenance (Fig. 51).

## Nano Banana

Google's "Nano Banana" – officially known as Gemini 2.5 Flash Image – is the latest AI model from Google for image generation and editing. It is a multimodal vision-language model that can take one or more input images plus text prompts, and produce new images by following the instructions. Unlike earlier image AIs, Nano Banana is designed for high fidelity output and fine-grained control. Its key capabilities include the ability to blend multiple input images into one, perform targeted edits via natural language (without needing any masks or manual selections), and preserve the consistency of subjects or designs across multiple images.

**Figure 51.** Moving geometric elements available on the Krea interface, and with live generation, Krea keeps creating variations. Users could play with the intensity of generation, colors, style, references, and much more. This is such a powerful tool to control what you want to edit and still see imaginative variations with AI.

**Key Features Relevant to Architects**

- **Text-Driven Edits (No Masks Needed):** Nano Banana allows architects to modify images using simple descriptions. You might say "replace the concrete facade with timber slats" or "add a soft shadow under the building's canopy", and the model will identify the facade or canopy in the image and make the change automatically. There's no need to draw masks or use Photoshop layers – the AI understands what you want to change and where to apply it, blending the edit seamlessly into the image. This is incredibly useful for trying out design tweaks (materials, lighting, landscaping, etc.) on a rendering without manual labor.
- **Consistent Design Across Iterations:** A major advantage of Nano Banana is its ability to maintain subject identity and scene details across multiple images or edits. If you generate a series of views of the same building, Nano Banana ensures the building remains the same in each image – it won't morph or change unintended features as you continue editing. Early testers have called it "the most consistent model" they've seen, noting that it can perform multi-step edits (changing several elements one after another) without "falling apart" or losing the design's integrity. For architects, this means you can keep refining one image (or creating new views) and trust that the core design – the building's form, details, and character – will persist across all the outputs.
- **Multi-Image Blending:** Nano Banana can take multiple input images and fuse them into a coherent new image. For example, you could provide a building rendering and a site photograph, and ask the model to place the designed building into that site context. The model will blend elements coherently, respecting lighting, perspective, and scale, so the result looks natural. This is useful for architects who want to compose scenes: you can combine a sketch, a reference image, and a material texture sample all in one go, and Nano Banana will generate a unified image that blends these sources (e.g., a conceptual collage or a realistic montage).
- **Localized Transformations via Natural Language:** The model excels at precise local edits directed by text prompts. You can target specific areas or elements with instructions, and Nano Banana figures out the rest. For instance, "make the lighting warmer on the east side of the building" or "remove that crane from the skyline" are instructions the AI can execute. It uses its understanding of the scene to apply changes only where appropriate (e.g., identifying the east facade, or detecting the crane to remove). This granular control means architects can fine-tune visuals (adjusting sunlight, swapping out sky conditions, editing foreground elements) just by typing requests.

- **High Fidelity & Style Versatility:** Despite the ease of use, Nano Banana produces high-quality, photorealistic renders on par with top image generators. It handles lighting and textures well, which is critical for believable architectural images. At the same time, it's versatile in style: you can ask for outputs ranging from a pencil sketch or watercolor illustration to a polished photorealistic image, and it will adapt accordingl. This means architects can generate both conceptual, stylized images and true-to-life visualizations from the same model, depending on the stage of design or the audience. For example, early in a project you might use a looser sketch style, and later switch to realistic mode for client presentations – all while keeping the underlying design consistent.

**Why Nano Banana is a Game-Changer for Architectural Design**

- **Rapid Iteration and Exploration:** Traditional rendering workflows are time-consuming – producing a single high-quality image can take hours, and making changes often means going back to the 3D model or manually editing in Photoshop. Nano Banana radically accelerates this process. Architects can iterate on a concept in near real-time by simply talking to the image. Imagine starting with an initial concept image and then guiding it step by step: "make the building 2 stories taller," "now change the facade to brick," "add trees and people in front," "turn the scene to dusk with warm light." With each instruction, the model updates the image accordingly, preserving the design's integrity throughout.
- **Consistency in Visual Series:** Architects rarely produce a single image; you typically need a series of visuals – exterior day and night views, interior shots, aerial perspectives, etc. – all depicting the same project. Ensuring consistency across these views (so the design reads the same in every image) is crucial and historically difficult with generative tools. Nano Banana's strength in preserving identities and scene context makes this much easier. You can generate several angles of a building and be confident that distinctive features (overall form, window patterns, materials) carry through each view. When you make an edit (say, change the roof material), the change appears in all subsequent renders of that project without the model unintentionally altering other parts of the scene. Early users noticed, for example, that Nano Banana keeps the camera perspective and lighting stable when asked – if you request a dusk version of a daytime render, it will shift the time of day while keeping the viewpoint and composition the same. This level of control is critical for realism and on-brand presentations, allowing architects to present a cohesive narrative of their design across multiple images.

- **Flexible Re-Visualization (Re-lighting, Re-materializing, Re-framing):** Because of its consistency and understanding of scenes, Nano Banana enables architects to take one design and re-visualize it in many ways without starting from scratch each time. The same project can be:
  - *Re-lit:* Change the lighting conditions (e.g. day to night, or overcast to sunny) with a prompt, to study the design in different atmospheres or highlight certain features at different times of day.
  - *Re-materialized:* Swap materials or colors on the design (e.g. *"make the exterior brick instead of concrete"*) and the model will apply the new material uniformly while respecting the building's form. This helps in exploring material options quickly.
  - *Re-framed:* Adjust the camera view or composition slightly – for instance, *"zoom in on the entrance"* or *"show the building from a pedestrian eye-level"*. Nano Banana can generate these new framings while keeping the building's geometry consistent. It even supports outpainting, meaning you can extend the borders of an image to reveal more context (widening a view) while matching the original perspective.

**Nano Banana session**

- Open Google AI Studio and select Gemini 2.5 Flash Image.
- Upload the Krea image as Image A.
- Optional: upload a roof or aerial reference as Image B if you intend to generate isometrics with a plausible top.
- In the instruction field, state roles and invariants, for example: "Use A for geometry and camera. Use B only for roof cues. Preserve massing and window rhythm. Maintain focal length 35 mm and camera height 1.6 m unless I ask otherwise."
- Generate a 45-degree isometric by asking:
- Generate a top view
- Generate a facade set by chaining local material and light edits on the same canvas.
- Create me an architectural representation layout with sections, elevations, sketches, plans, and isometry.
- Export each step so you have a clean sequence for critique and a record of prompt lineage (Fig. 52).
- Export the image created of the Isometric object into any 3d mesh generator (Fig. 53).

These tools open speed while loosening strict adherence to the initial mental image. Accept the trade in early design, where positive ambiguity

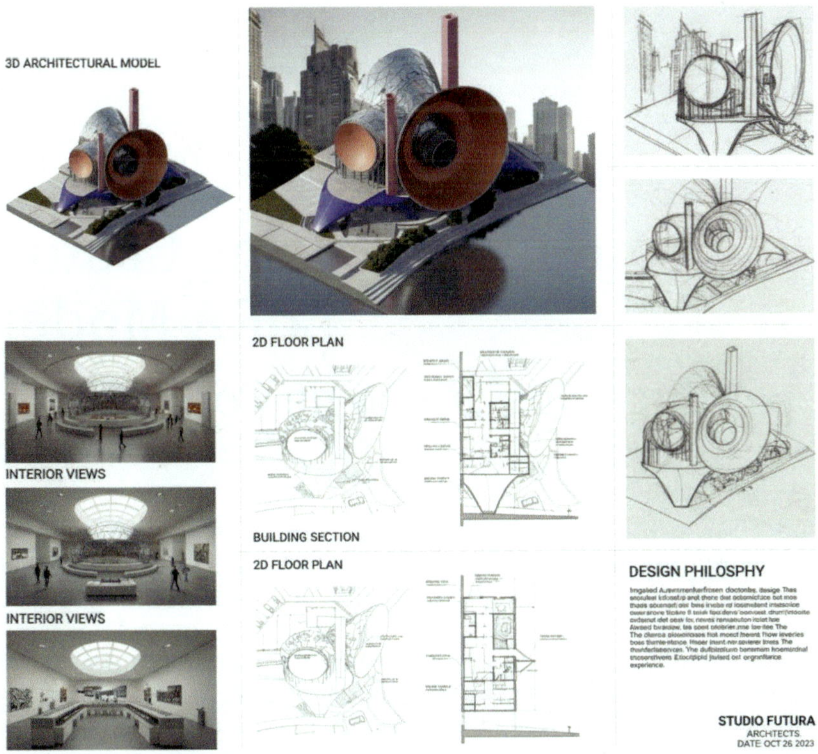


**Figure 52.** Complete architecture board created by Nano Banana.

is a resource for negotiation. Tighten constraints when you must preserve identity for decision making.

### MeshyAI

With MeshyAI after uploading the original created image, Meshy.ai created a detailed 3d out of it.

**Figure 53.** After the image created in Nano Banana was generated, the image was inserted into Meshy.AI as from personal experience, with the new Meshy 5 model, it gives one of the most detailed 3d mesh output.

Chapter 27

# Training and Using Custom LoRA Models

## Office-Specific Style Conditioning

Architectural practices often cultivate unique visual languages—certain formal tendencies, textures, atmospheres, and representational biases that distinguish one office's output from another. Yet most AI-generated imagery defaults to generic, internet-trained priors: highly stylized, occasionally exotic, and often inconsistent with an office's voice.

This chapter introduces Low-Rank Adaptation (LoRA) as a method to inject specificity into generative workflows. Rather than retraining a full model (which is GPU-intensive and time-consuming), LoRA enables targeted fine-tuning of a small subset of model weights, creating a light "adapter" that can be applied at generation time to steer output toward office-specific aesthetics.

### What is LoRA?

LoRA (Low-Rank Adaptation) is a method for fine-tuning large models using parameter-efficient training. Instead of updating all weights in the neural network, LoRA injects a small trainable matrix into specific layers—usually the attention or transformer layers of a diffusion model.

- Original model: remains untouched
- LoRA adapter: adds stylistic bias or domain-specific conditioning
- During inference: the adapter is merged temporarily with the base model

DOI: 10.1201/9781003637691-29

**Advantages:**

- Fast to train (minutes to hours)
- Requires far less GPU memory
- Doesn't overwrite the base model
- Multiple LoRAs can be swapped or blended

## Why LoRA Matters for Architects

- **Style Consistency**: Align generative outputs with your firm's visual language.
- **Portfolio Embedding**: Train on previous projects to reproduce that aesthetic in speculative images.
- **Team Coherence**: Ensure junior staff or students generate outputs that reflect senior design direction.
- **Client Alignment**: Generate proposals in a style your client has already approved.

## Preparing a LoRA Training Dataset

The most important factor in LoRA training is the curation of the training set.

**Requirements:**

- 20 to 200 images of past architectural projects or representations
- Consistent resolution (usually 512x512 or 768x768) - is a good recommendation for balancing quality and training speed. A higher resolutions is possible but require more resources.
- Consistent naming scheme (for captioning)
- Optionally: text captions describing each image's style or content

**Example Image Set:**

- A selection of renders from a firm's past competitions
- Scanned hand drawings with a distinctive line quality
- Diagrams with a recognizable visual logic (e.g. MVRDV, BIG, SANAA)

Avoid including images with wildly different styles; the adapter will overfit or fail to generalize.

## LoRA Training Tools and Pipelines

As of mid-2025, the most accessible tools for LoRA training include:

- **Kohya Trainer**: GUI-based, popular for image-to-LoRA workflows
- **Diffusers + PEFT (HuggingFace)**: Python-based, for advanced users
- **InvokeAI and Automatic1111 extensions**: offer plug-in trainers

Once trained, the .safetensors file for the LoRA can be imported into ComfyUI using:

- LoRA Loader node
- Connect to the UNet and TextEncoder ports

In most pipelines, this connects directly after the Load Checkpoint node and before KSampler.

## Using Trained LoRA Models in ComfyUI

Once loaded, your LoRA adapter influences the generation like an aesthetic lens.

**Prompt Example:**

- Base: *"An art museum with floating concrete slabs and interior courtyards"*
- With LoRA: *Same prompt + internal visual logic from trained portfolio*

**LoRAs can also be combined or weighted:**

- LoRA A (30%) + LoRA B (70%) → blended outputs
- Negative LoRA weights can "remove" a style (experimental)

Use LoRA Stack nodes in ComfyUI for combining multiple adapters.

## Architectural Use Cases

- **Competition Proposals**: Generate entries in your office's visual tone
- **Client Prototypes**: Present alternate massings or interiors while maintaining firm identity
- **Academic Studios**: Train class-wide LoRA models to generate work in a common theme
- **Portfolio Augmentation**: Reimagine older projects in current styles for continuity

## Risks and Ethical Considerations

- **Overfitting**: Too few images = bad generalization
- **Visual Inbreeding**: Relying solely on LoRA-trained styles may stifle innovation
- **Bias Encoding**: If training data lacks diversity, outputs may replicate those limitations
- **Authorship Concerns**: Training on third-party images raises questions of aesthetic appropriation

**Mitigate these by:**

- Combining LoRA with prompt diversity
- Transparently documenting your dataset sources
- Avoiding training on copyrighted material without license

## Conclusion

LoRA models are the architectural equivalent of custom rendering templates, they allow firms, studios, or individuals to inject identity into AI outputs, making generative tools more than generic visualizers. As architectural production moves toward hybrid workflows, LoRA enables continuity, authorship, and coherence across generation.

# Chapter 28

# Preparing AI Outputs for VR and AR

## Toward Immersive Architectural Workflows

AI-generated imagery is often regarded as a final representational artifact—a static frame capturing mood, materiality, and composition. However, in speculative or experiential architectural practices, these images can serve as precursors to immersive environments. This chapter explores how outputs from ComfyUI can be strategically transformed for Virtual Reality (VR), Augmented Reality (AR), and Extended Reality (XR) applications.

The goal is not to simulate physical reality, but to construct atmospheres, test experiential sequences, and scaffold speculative spatialities from latent visual logic.

### From Latent Image to Spatial Envelope

ComfyUI does not output geometry, yet its images encode implicit spatial information:

- Depth cues and shadow logic
- Material and texture inference
- Spatial enclosure and occupation

By treating the AI image as a perceptual scaffold, we can extend its representational reach into:

- 360° vc nbimmersive panoramas
- VR design sketches

DOI: 10.1201/9781003637691-30

- AR overlays on physical models
- Pseudo-3D parallax environments
- Volumetric approximations

## Workflow 1: 360° Panoramas for Immersive Visualization

The most accessible method for VR integration is the generation of equirectangular panoramas—images mapped to a 360° sphere for head-tracked navigation.

**Steps:**

1. **Prompt Engineering in ComfyUI**
   Example: *"Interior of a vaulted cathedral, equirectangular projection, 360°, VR rendering"*
2. **Set Aspect Ratio to 2:1**
   Use resolutions like 1024×512, 2048×1024, or higher.
3. **Enable panoramic rendering**
   Insert a 360°/equirectangular projection node set (e.g., Latent-to-Equirectangular/Spherical Projection from a 360-capable node pack) on the latent path feeding KSampler. Keep the canvas 2:1 (e.g., 2048×1024). The usual placement is after Load Checkpoint/VAE Encode (or Empty Latent Image) and before KSampler, so the UNet operates in an equirectangular/spherical domain. Decode as usual with VAE Decode.
4. **Import into VR platforms**
   Compatible with:
   - Unity (as Skybox)
   - Oculus Media Player
   - WebVR tools (A-Frame, Three.js)

**Use Case:** Immersive design reviews where users can *"step inside"* an architectural mood or conceptual space.

## Workflow 2: Depth Map Parallax for Pseudo-3D

ComfyUI can generate depth information using built-in estimators like MiDaS, ZoeDepth, or LeReS. These depth maps can be used to simulate spatial depth through displacement or parallax shaders.

**Steps:**

1. Generate a RGB + Depth Map pair in ComfyUI:
   - Nodes: KSampler → MidasDepthEstimator/ZoeDepth

2. Import into:
   - Blender: for parallax displacement on geometry
   - Three.js: for interactive web visualization
   - Depthy or MapBox Vision: for web/mobile depth illusions
3. Apply parallax or displacement shaders to create pseudo-3D motion

Limitation: This method creates visual illusion, not real 3D space. It is excellent for walkthrough prototypes or scroll-responsive spatial animations.

## Workflow 3: AR Integration Using Visual Anchors

Architects can project AI-generated atmospheres into physical contexts using marker-based or markerless AR.

Methods:

- **Marker-based AR (e.g., QR, Fiducials)**

  Platforms: Spark AR, Vuforia, Adobe Aero

  Attach AI imagery to physical anchors (walls, models, QR codes)
- **Projection Mapping**

  Use AI renderings to animate physical models with mapped light and shadow
- **AR with Spatial Anchors**

  Align AI-generated scenes with real-world coordinates (e.g., Hololens, iPad LiDAR)

**Use Case:** A student displays a cardboard model of a housing block. With AR, AI-generated cladding styles or lighting sequences are projected *onto* the model using a tablet or headset.

## Workflow 4: Hybrid Environments with AI + Procedural Geometry

To move closer toward volumetric experience, one can combine abstract geometry from Rhino/Grasshopper with AI-generated imagery as texture, skybox, or HDRI backdrop.

**Steps:**

1. Export AI image from ComfyUI
2. In Blender or Unity:
   - Map the image to geometry (façade, ground plane, or as a dome)
   - Match lighting and perspective using AI horizon cues

3. Add navigation or interaction layer:
   - o Simple camera walkthroughs
   - o Triggered mood swaps via image blends

This method is not photorealistic, but powerful in early-stage immersive storytelling—allowing clients or jurors to "walk through" an idea before formal modeling.

## Spatial Coherence Tips and Pitfalls

- **Perspective Alignment**: Match vanishing points for compositional realism
- **Human Scale**: Reference human proportions in prompt (or use ControlNet skeletons)
- **Avoid Lens Distortion**: Use panoramic or orthographic prompts to maintain coherence
- **Match Resolutions**: Keep image and depth resolutions aligned to avoid shader glitches
- **Segment Interiors**: Use masks to separate floors, ceilings, and furniture for better AR placement

## Future Outlook: Toward AI-Native XR

While ComfyUI is not natively 3D-aware, open-source tools are emerging that may soon allow for AI-native XR workflows:

- **Neural Radiance Fields (NeRFs):** Generate volumetric fields from multi-view image sets
- **3D Gaussian Splatting:** Real-time rendering of point-based environments from AI + camera sources (Luma AI, SplatFusion)
- **Multi-View ComfyUI Scripts:** Generate consistent front/side/top views for NeRF bootstrapping
- **LoRA/IPAdapter Fusion for Scene Matching:** Style-match across camera angles

As of July 2025, these are external integrations, not internal to ComfyUI—but they signal the emergent fusion of latent synthesis and volumetric computing.

ComfyUI's image generation should not be confined to screens. When embedded into XR pipelines, it becomes a speculative atmosphere engine, providing architects with the capacity to test, exhibit, and inhabit visual thought. These workflows reanimate the drawing with presence, converting it into space. In doing so, AI becomes not a visual crutch, but a portal, from rendering to inhabitation (Fig. 54).

**Figure 54.** During my class of Designing with artificial intelligence, together with Prof. Nadine Zinser-Junghanns introducing VR to students after inserting a 3d mesh into the machine.

# Chapter 29

# Troubleshooting and Optimizing ComfyUI Workflows for Architectural Image Quality

Even with a well-structured pipeline, issues inevitably emerge in generative design workflows—especially when architectural fidelity, material coherence, and stylistic precision are desired. This chapter provides a clear troubleshooting guide along with optimization strategies tailored to ComfyUI, specifically for architectural design use cases.

## Common Image Quality Issues

1. **Blurry or Muddled Detail**

- Cause: Low-resolution initialization, insufficient sampling steps, or weak CFG guidance.
- Solution:
  - o Increase resolution using EmptyLatentImage to 1024×1024 or higher.
  - o Raise sampling steps in KSampler (try 40–60 for mid-quality, 80–100 for high detail).
  - o Use a high-fidelity upscaler (4x-UltraSharp, RealESRGAN, or LatentUpscale) post-generation.

2. **Overexposure or Underexposure**

- Cause: Misaligned CFG values, model bias in light rendering, or inadequate VAE decoding.

DOI: 10.1201/9781003637691-31

- Solution:
  - Adjust brightness and contrast using ColorCorrection or ImageAdjustment nodes.
  - Lower CFG Scale slightly (to 6–7) to reduce prompt over-dominance in illumination logic.
  - Consider switching VAEs or using an EnhancedVAEDecode node if available.

3. **Color Inconsistency Across Frames (Video)**

- Cause: Inconsistent seeds, prompt drift, or unanchored interpolation.
- Solution:
  - Lock seeds across frame generations.
  - Use LatentInterpolator (instead of direct frame synthesis) to smooth transitions.
  - Fix VAE model and sampler settings across time.

## Structural and Geometric Failures

1. **Object Distortions (Melting, Warping)**

- Cause: Weak architectural prompts or unconditioned generation.
- Solution:
  - Use ControlNet (Canny or Depth) with clear structural input.
  - Reduce sampling randomness (switch to DPM++ 2M Karras).
  - Try enabling High CFG Precision or Hybrid Samplers where available.

2. **Loss of Design Coherence in Iteration**

- Cause: Over-randomization or prompt inconsistency.
- Solution:
  - Use Fixed Seed values or save Latent tensors for re-injection.
  - Chain prompts using IPAdapter or ReferenceOnly to maintain stylistic identity.

## Prompt-Related Errors

1. **Prompt Overload (Too Many Descriptors)**

- Cause: Excessive comma-separated elements create incoherent output.

- Solution:
  - Isolate architectural priorities. Instead of:

    *"Modern brutalist villa, white concrete, full glass facade, ocean view, metal balustrades, rooftop pool"*, try:

    *"Brutalist villa with full glass facade and rooftop pool."*

2. **Prompt Misunderstanding**

- Cause: Model fails to interpret architectural jargon.
- Solution:
  - Rephrase technically obscure terms.

    "Clerestory window" → "high narrow window near roofline" "Fenestration" → "window pattern"

## Optimization Strategies for Architectural Rendering

A. **Sampling Techniques**

- Steps (Denoising Iterations)
  - Use **50–80 steps** for static scenes with complex textures.
  - Use **100+** only when absolute realism is needed and compute allows.
- Sampler Selection
  - **DPM++ 2M Karras**: Best for edge definition and light balance (architecture default).
  - **Euler A**: Fast but unstable—use for quick drafts only.
  - **DDIM / Heun**: Balanced output for interior lighting effects.
- CFG Scale Tuning
  - Keep between 6.5–8.5 for architectural scenes.

    Too low → weak structure; too high → overfit hallucination.

B. **Resolution and Framing**

- **Start Large, Then Downscale**

  Render at 1536×1024 or 2048×1536, then reduce via ResizeImage or in Photoshop for cleaner edges.
- Aspect Ratio Logic
  - **16:9** → urban exteriors or horizontal compositions
  - **1:1** → material studies, facade elements
  - **9:16** → towers, section perspectives, mobile layouts

**C. Enhancements and Post-Processing**

- Denoising

  Apply ImageDenoise node to smooth out high-frequency noise after upscale or mask edits.

- Sharpness

  Use SharpenImage, or external tools like Topaz Labs for final tweaks.

- Color Balance

  Use ImageAdjustment or external tools like Lightroom to match desired presentation mood.

## Efficient Architectural Workflow Practices

- **Save Workflows as JSON Presets**

  Export ComfyUI node graphs for repeatable architectural styles:

  - "Post-industrial site axonometry"
  - "Vernacular school courtyard"
  - "Tectonic detail shadows"

- **Use LatentSaver/Loader**

  This allows iterative development from the same latent base—key in phased design.

- **Batching with BatchPrompt or PromptMatrix**

  Automate variation generation: material options, lighting variants, programmatic changes.

- **Track Prompt Iterations**

  Use metadata tools (SavePromptInfo) or embed parameters in filenames for later comparison.

## Diagram: Robust ComfyUI Pipeline (2025 Best Practice)

*Suggestion*: A flowchart diagram illustrating:

- Input Nodes → Prompt + ControlNet + IPAdapter
- → Latent Init → KSampler → Latent Save
- → VAE Decode → Color/Sharpness Nodes
- → SaveImage + Metadata Save

Chapter 30

# Useful Shortcuts for ComfyUI

| Keybind | Explanation |
|---|---|
| Ctrl + Enter | Queue up current graph for generation |
| Ctrl + Shift + Enter | Queue up current graph as first for generation |
| Ctrl + Alt + Enter | Cancel current generation |
| Ctrl + Z/Ctrl + Y | Undo/Redo |
| Ctrl + S | Save workflow |
| Ctrl + O | Load workflow |
| Ctrl + A | Select all nodes |
| Alt + C | Collapse/uncollapse selected nodes |
| Ctrl + M | Mute/unmute selected nodes |
| Ctrl + B | Bypass selected nodes (acts like the node was removed from the graph and the wires reconnected through) |
| Delete/Backspace | Delete selected nodes |
| Ctrl + Backspace | Delete the current graph |
| Space | Move the canvas around when held and moving the cursor |
| Ctrl/Shift + Click | Add clicked node to selection |
| Ctrl + C/Ctrl + V | Copy and paste selected nodes (without maintaining connections to outputs of unselected nodes) |
| Ctrl + C/Ctrl + Shift + V | Copy and paste selected nodes (maintaining connections from outputs of unselected nodes to inputs of pasted nodes) |
| Shift + Drag | Move multiple selected nodes at the same time |
| Ctrl + D | Load default graph |
| Alt + + | Canvas Zoom in |
| Alt + - | Canvas Zoom out |
| Ctrl + Shift + LMB + Vertical drag | Canvas Zoom in/out |
| P | Pin/Unpin selected nodes |

DOI: 10.1201/9781003637691-32

| | |
|---|---|
| Ctrl + G | Group selected nodes |
| Q | Toggle visibility of the queue |
| H | Toggle visibility of history |
| R | Refresh graph |
| F | Show/Hide menu |
| . | Fit view to selection (Whole graph when nothing is selected) |
| Double-Click LMB | Open node quick search palette |
| Shift + Drag | Move multiple wires at once |
| Ctrl + Alt + LMB | Disconnect all wires from clicked slot |

Ctrl can also be replaced with Cmd instead for macOS users

# Conclusion

## From Latent Hallucinations to Architectural Epistemologies of Control

Our exploration began in the shadows of a medieval cathedral, contemplating the Master Mason whose craft and knowledge were inseparable from the act of creation. This historical figure stood at a pivotal crossroads when confronted by the transformative emergence of the architectural drawing—disegno—threatening to reduce his role from author to mere technician. That ancient tension, embodying the recurrent drama of technological disruption and the specter of professional displacement, has illuminated the intellectual trajectory of this volume. Today, we stand at our own historical inflection point, equipped not with simple instruments of representation, but with sophisticated tools of computational abstraction and probabilistic inference, far more potent and enigmatic than the parchment drawings that once revolutionized architectural authorship.

Throughout this book, we have navigated a dual path—from the theoretical foundations underpinning artificial intelligence to practical mastery of its technical intricacies. We established that AI introduces a paradigm shift in architectural technology, far surpassing earlier computational revolutions such as CAD and BIM. Scholars such as Mario Carpo (2011) and Antoine Picon (2010) have rightly emphasized that previous computational tools operated strictly within a deterministic logic, faithfully executing explicit instructions authored by the architect. In contrast, artificial intelligence inaugurates a fundamentally different epistemology: it operates not through explicit instructions, but through a logic of inference, creating an epistemic rupture unprecedented since the Renaissance.

AI does not merely digitize architectural drawings—it transforms them into latent spaces, vast multidimensional fields of probabilistic possibilities derived from patterns of collective visual culture. Architectural design,

DOI: 10.1201/9781003637691-33

within this context, becomes an act of navigation, an exploration within these rich latent territories, rather than a linear progression from first principles. We have argued throughout this book that architecture, thus, evolves into a dynamic feedback loop—a dialectical relationship between human intentionality and machine-generated statistical hallucinations.

At the core of our inquiry lies a crucial revaluation: the machine's hallucination, far from being an error or distortion, emerges as a novel material for design exploration. Controlling the hallucination, therefore, signifies a radical epistemic shift from passive reception to active cultivation, a conscious decision to navigate, shape, and direct the generative potential of AI. The practical chapters provided in this book—covering tools such as the node-based workflows of ComfyUI, the disciplined structural guidance of ControlNet, the stylistic coherence offered by IPAdapters, and the personalized identity achieved through LoRA models—are not merely technical methodologies; they represent essential navigational instruments for architects traversing this emergent, invisible landscape. They transform mere linguistic prompting into an inherently architectural act.

In acquiring mastery over these AI-driven processes, architects confront profound philosophical questions surrounding agency and authorship. In a scenario where architectural form emerges through co-creation with algorithmic systems, the classical notion of singular authorship requires redefinition. Rather than diminishing the architect's role, we have argued that authorship is enriched and expanded. The architect, in this augmented paradigm, evolves into a sophisticated system orchestrator: curating and selecting data, constructing generative workflows, and exercising critical discernment over AI-generated outcomes. This redefinition calls for philosophical vigilance—constant awareness of implicit biases embedded in datasets, an understanding of the limitations inherent in computational models, and acute sensitivity to the broader societal ramifications of AI-driven designs.

Moreover, our exploration gestures toward future horizons of architectural epistemology. Emerging technological integrations, such as real-time data assimilation, hybrid AI-parametric feedback mechanisms, and immersive virtual and augmented reality environments, reveal glimpses of an architectural intelligence that is inherently distributed, dynamically adaptive, and profoundly co-evolutionary. The future architect will no longer be confined to the mere creation of static objects; instead, they will engage in active dialogues with emergent spatial imaginaries, mediating human aspirations, environmental imperatives, and the alien logics of computational intelligence.

Thus, our journey—from mastering hallucinations to cultivating new epistemological practices—marks not a departure from architectural tradition but its radical reinvention. Much like Leon Battista Alberti redefined the architect as an intellectual distinct from the builder, today's architects must redefine themselves as epistemic mediators. This evolved professional identity requires dual literacies: fluency in the timeless humanistic languages of space, form, and experience, and fluency in the emergent languages of data, probability, and computational inference. By mastering this new art of hallucination, architects reclaim design as an integrated practice of technical rigor and philosophical depth. In an era characterized by dreaming machines, the architect's essential role is clear: to provide the compass, set the ethical and aesthetic course, and mediate meaningfully between humanity and algorithmic possibility.

# References


75F Building Intelligence System. [Internet]. 75F; [cited 2023]. Available from: https://www.75f.io/.

Adobe Inc. Adobe Firefly. [Internet]. [cited 2023]. Available from: https://www.adobe.com/products/firefly.html.

Adobe Photoshop (Beta). [Internet]. Adobe; [cited 2023]. Available from: https://www.adobe.com/products/photoshop.html.

al-Rawi, O. M. (2020). Origins of computational design in architecture. Future Engineering Journal, 1(1), Article 5. Retrieved from https://digitalcommons.aaru.edu.jo/fej/vol1/iss1/5

ALICE Technologies. [Internet]. [cited 2023]. Available from: https://www.alicetechnologies.com/.

Ang, K. M., El-kenawy, E.-S. M., Abdelhamid, A. A., Ibrahim, A., Alharbi, A. H., Khafaga, D. S. et al. (2022). Optimal design of convolutional neural network architectures using teaching–learning-based optimization for image classification. Symmetry, 14(11): 2323. https://doi.org/10.3390/sym14112323.

Arch Hive. (2022). AI Architecture Competition: Winter Fashion Store Winners. Retrieved from https://amazingarchitecture.com/news/ai-architecture-competition-2022-winners-announced?fbclid=PAZXh0bgNhZW0CMTEAAafNx_ac1rxoE-n0JFy_c7_1jHDEqW-_yd14F5gn0AcpcAd3v65E1lIe9S0ZQw_aem_2qNGyxZYNES4tE4PDKiKqA.

Arch Hive. (2023). AI Architecture Competition: Artificial Nature. Retrieved from https://amazingarchitecture.com/tags/hyejin-shin.

Archistar. [Internet]. [cited 2023]. Available from: https://www.archistar.ai/.

Architechtures. [Internet]. [cited 2023]. Available from: https://architechtures.com/en.

ARK. [Internet]. [cited 2023]. Available from: https://www.archisketch.com/.

ArkoAI. [Internet]. [cited 2023]. Available from: https://www.arko.ai/.

Autodesk Generative Design. [Internet]. [cited 2023]. Available from: https://www.autodesk.com/products/generative-design/overview?term=1-YEARandtab=subscription.

Autodesk Inc. Autodesk Forma. [Internet]. Autodesk; [cited 2023]. Available from: https://www.autodesk.com/products/forma/overview?term=1-YEARandtab=subscription.

Autodesk's Dreamcatcher. [Internet]. Autodesk; [cited 2023]. Available from: https://www.autodesk.com/products/dreamcatcher/overview.

Atelier Algorithmic Design. (2025). Real-world experiments. https://atelier.design/experiments.

Attashe. (n.d.). FluxRegionAttention: ComfyUI Screenshot 4 [Image]. GitHub. https://github.com/attashe/ComfyUI-FluxRegionAttention/blob/master/images/comfy_screenshot_4.png.

Barker, N. (2023). Hickok Cole uses ChatGPT to design 24-storey mixed-use building. Hickok Cole Lab. Retrieved from https://www.dezeen.com/2023/06/23/hickok-cole-chatgpt-aitopia/.

Blueprints AI. [Internet]. [cited 2023]. Available from: https://www.blueprints-ai.com/.

BricsCAD. [Internet]. Bricsys; [cited 2023]. Available from: https://www.bricsys.com/.
Briscoe, F., and Gardner, H. K. (2017). Richard Susskind and Daniel Susskind: The Future of the Professions: How Technology Will Transform the Work of Human Experts:. Administrative Science Quarterly, 62(4). Retrieved 1 1, 2025, from https://journals.sagepub.com/doi/abs/10.1177/0001839217716083.
Bronstein, M. M., Bruna, J., LeCun, Y., Szlam, A., and Vandergheynst, P. (2017). Geometric Deep Learning: Going beyond Euclidean data. IEEE Signal Processing Magazine, 34(4): 18–42.
Burry, J., and Burry, M. (2021). Prototyping for Architects: Real Buildings in a Virtual World. Routledge.
Bush, V. (1945). As we may think. The Atlantic Monthly, 176(1): 101–108.
Canvas. Canvas For Construction. [Internet]. Canvas; [cited 2023 July 26]. Available from: https://Www.Canvas.Build/.
Carpo, M. (2011). The Alphabet and the Algorithm. MIT Press.
Carpo, M. (2017). The second digital turn: Design beyond intelligence. Cambridge, MA: MIT Press.
Carpo, M. (2024). Perspectives in computational design: A brief assessment of today's socio-technical context, promises, and challenges. Perspectives in Architecture and Urbanism, 1(1): 100001. https://doi.org/10.1016/j.pau.2024.100001.
Chat GPT. [Internet]. OpenAI; [cited 2023]. Available from: https://chat.openai.com/.
Chatmind. [Internet]. [cited 2023]. Available from: https://chatmind.tech/.
Civils.ai. [Internet]. [cited 2023]. Available from: https://civils.ai/.
ClickUp. [Internet]. [cited 2023]. Available from: https://clickup.com/.
Collovgpt. [Internet]. [cited 2023]. Available from: https://collov.ai/.
ComfyUI Wiki. (2025a). How to use OpenPose ControlNet SD1.5 model in ComfyUI. https://comfyui-wiki.com/en/tutorial/advanced/how-to-use-openpose-controlnet-with-sd1.5.
ComfyUI Wiki. (2025b). Using ControlNet in ComfyUI for precise controlled image generation. https://comfyui-wiki.com/en/tutorial/advanced/how-to-install-and-use-controlnet-models-in-comfyui.
ComfyUI Wiki. (2025c). Wan2.1 ComfyUI workflow - Complete guide. https://comfyui-wiki.com/en/tutorial/advanced/video/wan2.1/wan2-1-video-model.
ComfyUI-Wiki. (2025). HunyuanVideo text-to-video workflow guide and examples. https://comfyui-wiki.com/en/tutorial/advanced/hunyuan-text-to-video-workflow-guide-and-example.
Construction Robotics. Sam100. [Internet]. Construction Robotics; [cited 2023 July 26]. Available from: https://Www.Construction-Robotics.Com/Sam100/.
Cove.tool. [Internet]. [cited 2023]. Available from: https://cove.tools/.
ComfyUI Community. (2024–2025). Official ComfyUI Discord server and extensions. https://discord.gg/comfyui.
Cybertect. (n.d.). Inpainting Flux (CropAndStitch). Civitai. https://civitai.com/models/510820/inpainting-flux-cropandstitch.
A deep dive into ControlNet and IPAdapter workflow. (2025). ComfyUI.org. https://comfyui.org/en/image-style-transfer-controlnet-ipadapter-workflow.
Designs.ai. [Internet]. [cited 2023]. Available from: https://www.designs.ai/.
Digital Blue Foam. [Internet]. [cited 2023]. Available from: https://www.digitalbluefoam.com/.
Docs.comfy.org. (2025a). ComfyUI depth ControlNet usage example. https://docs.comfy.org/tutorials/controlnet/depth-controlnet.
Docs.comfy.org. (2025b). ComfyUI pose ControlNet usage example. https://docs.comfy.org/tutorials/controlnet/pose-controlnet-2-pass.
Eastman, C. (1975). The use of computers instead of drawings in building design. Proceedings of the 1975 IFIP Congress, 1065–1072.

El Moussaoui, M., and Krois, K. (2024). Architectural pedagogy in the age of AI: The transformation of a domain. *In*: Barosio, M., Vigliocco, E., and Gomes, S. (Eds.). School of Architecture(s) - New Frontiers of Architectural Education Springer.

El Moussaoui, M. (2024). Architectural Typology and its Influence on Authentic Living. Buildings, 14: 754. https:// doi.org/10.3390/buildings14030754.

El Moussaoui, M. (2024). Aesthetics, Authenticity & City place-making. Rivista di Estetica. *In*: Armando, A. and Siddi, N. (Eds.). The Philosophy of the City. ISBN 9791259933119 (print). 85, 216.

El Moussaoui, M. (2025a). Artificial Intelligence: Beyond Ocularcentrism, the New Age of Humans Beyond the Spectacle. pp. 35–47. *In*: El Moussaoui, M., Krois, K. and Palmiere, T. (Eds.). Power in Transformation. OEKOM. ISBN 978-3-98726-150-3.

El Moussaoui, M. (2025b). Architectural practice process and artificial intelligence: A review on an evolving practice. Open Engineering, 15(1): 20240098. https://doi.org/10.1515/eng-2024-0098.

El Moussaoui, M. (2025c). Redefining Authorship in Architecture in the Age of AI. *In*: Philipp Hacker (ed.). Oxford Intersections: AI in Society (Oxford, online edn, Oxford Academic, 20 Mar. 2025), https://doi.org/10.1093/9780198945215.003.0033.

El Moussaoui, M. (2025d). Future Illiteracies—Architectural Epistemology and Artificial Intelligence. Architecture, 5(3), 53. https://doi.org/10.3390/architecture5030053.

Encarnação, J. L., Lindner, R., and Schlechtendahl, E. G. (1990). History and basic components of CAD. *In*: Computer Aided Design. Symbolic Computation. Springer, Berlin, Heidelberg. https://doi.org/10.1007/978-3-642-84054-8_2.

Exyn Technologies. [Internet]. [cited 2023]. Available from: https://www.exyn.com/.

Fabrie. [Internet]. [cited 2023]. Available from: https://www.fabrie.com/home.

Finch3d. [Internet]. [cited 2023]. Available from: https://www.finch3d.com/.

Food4Rhino. (n.d.). ComfyUI for Rhino and Grasshopper. Retrieved August 4, 2025, from https://www.food4rhino.com/en/app/comfyui-rhino-grasshopper.

Formica. (2023). A brief history of AI (artificial intelligence). https://www.formica.ai/blog/brief-history-of-ai-artificial-intelligence (Accessed. July 2024).

Frazer, J. (1995). An Evolutionary Architecture. Architectural Association.

Fulhaus Ludwig. [Internet]. [cited 2023]. Available from: https://www.fulhaus.com/meet-ludwig.

Flux-ML. (n.d.). FluxRegionAttention [GitHub repository]. GitHub. https://github.com/flux-ml/FluxRegionAttention.

Guo, Y. [guoyww]. (n.d.). AnimateDiff Regional Prompt [GitHub repository]. GitHub. https://github.com/guoyww/animatediff.

Gero, J. S. (1983). Computer-aided architectural design-past, present, future, Architectural Science Review 26(1): 2–5.

Getfloorplan. [Internet]. [cited 2023]. Available from: https://getfloorplan.com/?ref=deepgramandutm_source=deepgramandutm_medium=referral.

Goodacre, C. J., Kattadiyil, M. T., and Rungcharassaeng, A. S. (2012). CAD/CAM fabricated complete dentures: Concepts and clinical methods of obtaining required morphological data. The Journal of Prosthetic Dentistry, 107(1): 34–46. https://doi.org/10.1016/S0022-3913(12)60024-3.

Goodfellow, I., Pouget-Abadie, J., Mirza, M., Xu, B., Warde-Farley, D., Ozair, S. et al. (2014). Generative adversarial nets. Advances in Neural Information Processing Systems, 27.

Goodfellow, I., Bengio, Y., and Courville, A. (2016). Deep Learning. MIT Press.

Grasshopper3D. (n.d.). Firefly plugin group. Retrieved August 4, 2025, from https://www.grasshopper3d.com/group/fireflyplugin.

Gugerty, L. (2006). Newell and Simon's Logic Theorist: Historical background and impact on cognitive modeling. In Proceedings of the Human Factors and Ergonomics Society Annual Meeting (Vol. 50, No. 9, pp. 880–884). https://doi.org/10.1177/154193120605000904.

Hestyaai. [Internet]. [cited 2023]. Available from: https://www.hestyadesign.com/.
Hochreiter, S., and Schmidhuber, J. (1997). Long short-term memory. Neural Computation, 9(8): 1735–1780.
HomeByMe. [Internet]. [cited 2023]. Available from: https://home.by.me/.
Homedesignai. [Internet]. [cited 2023]. Available from: https://homedesigns.ai/?gad_source=1andgclid=CjwKCAiArLyuBhA7EiwA-qo80GcUeX1XAnxu3wDS3ccHH7z0VZhuw1CmcCg7jebIyD8nw5bR8_CkNRoCDsoQAvD_BwE.
Homestyler. [Internet]. [cited 2023]. Available from: https://www.homestyler.com/.
Hugging Face. (2025). IP-Adapter documentation. https://huggingface.co/docs/diffusers/using-diffusers/ip_adapter.
Hutch. [Internet]. [cited 2023]. Available from: https://hutchdesign.co/.
Hypar.ai. [Internet]. [cited 2023]. Available from: https://hypar.io/.
IKEA Place. [Internet]. [cited 2023]. Available from: https://www.ikea.com/us/en/.
Interiorai. [Internet]. [cited 2023]. Available from: https://www.interiorai.com/.
Interview Kickstart. (2025). Automating data workflows with AI prompt engineering. https://interviewkickstart.com/blogs/learn/automating-data-workflows-ai-prompt-engineering.
IPAdapter tutorial. (2024). Comflowy. https://www.comflowy.com/blog/IPAdapter-Tutorial.
Kalay, Y. E. (2004). Architecture's New Media: Principles, Theories, and Methods of Computer-Aided Design. MIT Press.
Kelleher, J. D. (2019). Deep Learning. MIT Press.
Kreo. [Internet]. [cited 2023]. Available from: https://www.kreo.net/.
Krizhevsky, A., Sutskever, I., and Hinton, G. E. (2012). ImageNet Classification with Deep Convolutional Neural Networks. Communications of the ACM.
Kofler, I., El Moussaoui, M., and Jamet, R. (2024). AI's influence on the creative and cultural industries. Imago, 13(24).
Laiserin, J. (2002). Comparing Pommes and Naranjas. The Laiserin Letter, 15.
Le Corbusier. (2007). Towards a New Architecture. Getty Research Institute. (Original work published 1923).
LeCun, Y., Boser, B., Denker, J. S., Henderson, D., Howard, R. E., Hubbard, W. et al. (1989). Handwritten digit recognition with a back-propagation network. pp. 396–404. *In*: Touretzky, D. S. (Ed.). Advances in Neural Information Processing Systems (Vol. 2).
LEO. [Internet]. [cited 2023]. Available from: https://www.getleo.ai/.
LexSet. [Internet]. [cited 2023]. Available from: https://www.lexset.ai/.
Liang, J., Zhong, X., Zhao, S., Fricker, P., and Koh, I. (2025). Building-graph-AI: Graph neural networks learning and generating 3D detailed and layered building models. International Journal of Architectural Computing, 0(0). https://doi.org/10.1177/14780771251352946.
Lookx. [Internet]. [cited 2023]. Available from: https://lookx.ai/.
Maket. [Internet]. [cited 2023]. Available from: https://www.maket.ai/.
McCarthy, J., Minsky, M., Rochester, N., and Shannon, C. (1956). A Proposal for the Dartmouth Summer Research Project on Artificial Intelligence. Dartmouth College.
McLuhan, M. (1964). Understanding Media: The Extensions of Man. McGraw-Hill.
Midjourney. Midjourney. [Internet]. Available from: https://www.midjourney.com/. Accessed on 26/07/2023.
Mildenhall, B., Srinivasan, P. P., Tancik, M., Barron, J. T., Ramamoorthi, R., and Ng, R. (2020). NeRF: Representing scenes as neural radiance fields for view synthesis. European Conference on Computer Vision.
Mitchell, T. M. (1997). Machine Learning. McGraw-Hill.
Mitchell, W. J. (1990). The Logic of Architecture: Design, Computation, and Cognition. MIT Press.
Mnml.ai. [Internet]. [cited 2023]. Available from: https://mnml.ai/.

Monge, G. (2001). Descriptive Geometry. Dover Publications. (Original work published 1798).

MULE (Construction Robot). [Internet]. Construction Robotics; [cited 2023]. Available from: https://www.construction-robotics.com/mule/.

MX3D. [Internet]. [cited 2023]. Available from: https://mx3d.com/.

Negroponte, N. (1970). The Architecture Machine. MIT Press.

nTopology. [Internet]. [cited 2023]. Available from: https://www.ntop.com/.

OpenAI. [Internet]. Available from: https://openai.com/. Accessed on 26/07/2025.

OpenArt. (n.d.). Real-time architecture design | ComfyUI workflow. Retrieved August 4, 2025, from https://openart.ai/workflows/ghroth/real-time-architecture-design/XQiMHIcNDLbGiR6YmVYH.

Panofsky, E. (1991). Perspective as Symbolic Form. Zone Books.

Peters, A (2023, July 4). Could Your Next Office Building Be Designed by Artificial Intelligence? This Firm Tries to Find Out. Costar. Retrieved from https://www.costar.com/article/1093838167/could-your-next-office-building-be-designed-by-artificial-intelligence-this-firm-tries-to-find-out.

Picon, A. (2010). Digital Culture in Architecture: An Introduction for the Design Professions. Birkhäuser.

Pixel Easel. [Pixel Easel]. (2024, May 10). ComfyUI - Understanding denoise strength, CFG scale, steps, and model checkpoints [Video]. YouTube. https://www.youtube.com/watch?v=-YztmpHp8UA.

Price, C. (1971). Fun Palace Project. Architectural Review.

Programa. [Internet]. [cited 2023]. Available from: https://programa.design/features/?utm_term=interior%20design%20softwareandutm_campaign={campaignname}andutm_source=adwordandutm_medium=ppcandhsa_acc=6378901762andhsa_cam=20448274548andhsa_grp=153138031155andhsa_ad=669709968945andhsa_src=gandhsa_tgt=kwd-30660813andhsa_kw=interior%20design%20softwareandhsa_mt=pandhsa_net=adwordsandhsa_ver=3andgad_source=1andgclid=CjwKCAiArLyuBhA7EiwA-qo80EGXXRQt7NY4ibdOUXe79opEWFJAxP7vVKu72CgXce_8bFcv_s-1TRoCewIQAvD_BwE.

PromeAI. [Internet]. [cited 2023]. Available from: https://prome.ai/.

Qi, C. R., Yi, L., Su, H., and Guibas, L. J. (2017). PointNet++: Deep hierarchical feature learning on point sets in a metric space. NeurIPS 2017.

Radford, A., Kim, J. W., Hallacy, C., Ramesh, A., Goh, G., Agarwal, S. et al. (2021). Learning transferable visual models from natural language supervision. Proceedings of the 38th International Conference on Machine Learning.

ReimagineHome. [Internet]. [cited 2023]. Available from: https://reimaginehome.ai/.

ReRender.ai. [Internet]. [cited 2023]. Available from: https://rerenderai.com/?gad_source=1andgclid=CjwKCAiArLyuBhA7EiwA-qo80AlaDiW-j6gL_y3__mePAxUENIwcGG1FmL_y9POOvZTgW8XJuWJdKRoCTQ8QAvD_BwE.

ReRoom. [Internet]. [cited 2023]. Available from: https://www.reroom.ai/.

Rombach, R., Blattmann, A., Lorenz, D., Esser, P., and Ommer, B. (2022). High-resolution image synthesis with latent diffusion models. Proceedings of the IEEE/CVF Conference on Computer Vision and Pattern Recognition.

RoomGPT. [Internet]. [cited 2023]. Available from: https://www.roomsgpt.io/ai-interior-design.

Rosenblatt, F. (1958). The perceptron: A probabilistic model for information storage and organization in the brain. Psychological Review, 65(6): 386–408.

Rumelhart, D. E., Hinton, G. E., and Williams, R. J. (1986). Learning representations by back-propagating errors. Nature, 323(6088): 533–536.

RunComfy. (2024). Mastering ComfyUI ControlNet: A complete guide. https://www.runcomfy.com/tutorials/mastering-controlnet-in-comfyui.

RunComfy. (2025a). ComfyUI IPAdapter plus deep dive tutorial. https://www.runcomfy.com/tutorials/comfyui-ipadapter-plus-deep-dive-tutorial.
RunComfy. (2025b). ComfyUI node: Calculate normal map. https://www.runcomfy.com/comfyui-nodes/ComfyUI-Gaffer/CalculateNormalMap.
RunComfy. (2025c). ComfyUI node: Normal map lighting. https://www.runcomfy.com/comfyui-nodes/ComfyUI_yanc/--Normal-Map-Lighting.
RunComfy. (2025d). ComfyUI node: Text to video. https://www.runcomfy.com/comfyui-nodes/ComfyUI-LumaAI-API/LumaText2Video.
RunComfy. (2025e). Create 3D content with stable fast 3D model. RunComfy.
Runway.ai. [Internet]. [cited 2023]. Available from: https://runwayml.com/.
Russell, S., and Norvig, P. (2021). Artificial Intelligence: A Modern Approach (4th ed.). Pearson.
Rykwert, J. (1996). The Idea of a Town: The Anthropology of Urban Form in Rome, Italy and the Ancient World. MIT Press.
Scheeren, R. and LIMA, D. L. C. 2015. The Parametricism manifest: prospects about a "newglobal style" for architectural design and urban planning. V!RUS, São Carlos, n. 11.
Schumacher, P. (2008). Parametricism as Style—Parametricist Manifesto. 11th Venice Architecture Biennale.
Schumacher, P. (2010). Parametricism: A New Global Style for Architecture and Urban Design. AD Architectural Design, 79(4): 14–23.
Shakker.ai. (2025). Mastering ComfyUI ControlNet: Models, workflow, and examples. https://wiki.shakker.ai/en/comfyui-controlnet.
Shelden, D. (2002). Digital Surface Representation and the Constructibility of Gehry's Architecture. PhD Dissertation, Massachusetts Institute of Technology.
Sidewalk Labs. [Internet]. [cited 2023]. Available from: https://www.sidewalklabs.com/.
Sloyd. [Internet]. [cited 2023]. Available from: https://www.sloyd.ai/.
SmartDraw. [Internet]. [cited 2023]. Available from: https://www.smartdraw.com/.
Spacely. [Internet]. [cited 2023]. Available from: https://spacely.ai/.
Spoak. [Internet]. [cited 2023]. Available from: https://www.spoak.com/.
Susskind, R., and Susskind, D. (2015). The future of the professions: How technology will transform the work of human experts. Oxford University Press.
Sutherland, I. E. (1963). Sketchpad: A Man-Machine Graphical Communication System. Proceedings of the AFIPS Spring Joint Computer Conference, 329–346.
Sutton, R. S., and Barto, A. G. (2018). Reinforcement Learning: An Introduction (2nd ed.). MIT Press.
Swapp. [Internet]. [cited 2023]. Available from: https://www.swapp.ai/.
TestFit. [Internet]. Available from: https://testfit.io/. Accessed on 26/07/2023.
Toolify.ai. (2025). ComfyUI: Unleashing inpainting with Scribble ControlNet. https://www.toolify.ai/ai-news/comfyui-unleashing-inpainting-with-scribble-controlnet-3371400.
ToTree. [Internet]. [cited 2023]. Available from: https://totree.co/.
Turing, A. M. (1950). Computing Machinery and Intelligence. Retrieved 1 2, 2025, from https://link.springer.com/chapter/10.1007/978-1-4020-6710-5_3.
Undale, K. [Kedar Undale]. (2026, June). *Geometry to Render - Comfy x Grasshopper3D Tutorial Part 4* [Video]. YouTube. https://www.youtube.com/watch?v=dMZNWjTAOlU.
Varys. [Internet]. [cited 2023]. Available from: https://varys.ai/?lang=en.
Vaswani, A., Shazeer, N., Parmar, N., Uszkoreit, J., Jones, L., Gomez, A. N. et al. (2017). Attention is all you need. Advances in Neural Information Processing Systems, 30.
Veras. [Internet]. EvolveLAB; [cited 2023]. Available from: https://www.evolvelab.io/veras.
Visualise.ai. [Internet]. [cited 2023]. Available from: https://visualizeai.pro/.
Xkool. [Internet]. [cited 2023]. Available from: https://www.xkool.ai/.

Xu, H., Chang, R., Pan, M., Li, H., Liu, S., Webber, R. J. et al. (2022). Application of Artificial Neural Networks in Construction Management: A Scientometric Review. Buildings, 12(7): 952. https://doi.org/10.3390/buildings12070952.

Youns, A. M., and Grchev, K. (2024). A Historical and Critical Assessment of Parametricism as an Architectural Style in the 21st Century. Buildings, 14(9): 2656. https://doi.org/10.3390/buildings14092656.

Zeng, A., Song, S., Nießner, M., Fisher, M., Xiao, J., and Funkhouser, T. (2023). 3D Scene Transformers: Learning 3D Scene Generation with Transformers. IEEE Transactions on Pattern Analysis and Machine Intelligence.

# Index

## E



## G



## H



## I



## K



## L



## M



## N



## O



## P



## R



## S



## T

## U



## V

For Product Safety Concerns and Information please contact our EU representative GPSR@taylorandfrancis.com Taylor & Francis Verlag GmbH, Kaufingerstraße 24, 80331 München, Germany